THE AMAZON

OXFORD

THE AMAZON
Land Without History

Euclides da Cunha

Translated from the Portuguese by
RONALD SOUSA

Edited with Introduction and Notes by
LÚCIA SÁ

OXFORD
UNIVERSITY PRESS
2006

OXFORD
UNIVERSITY PRESS

Oxford University Press, Inc., publishes works that further
Oxford University's objective of excellence in research, scholarship, and education.

Oxford New York
Auckland Cape Town Dar es Salaam Hong Kong Karachi Kuala Lumpur Madrid
Melbourne Mexico City Nairobi New Delhi Shanghai Taipei Toronto

With offices in
Argentina Austria Brazil Chile Czech Republic France Greece
Guatemala Hungary Italy Japan Poland Portugal Singapore
South Korea Switzerland Thailand Turkey Ukraine Vietnam

Copyright © 2006 by Oxford University Press, Inc.

Published by Oxford University Press, Inc.
198 Madison Avenue, New York, NY 10016
www.oup.com

Oxford is a registered trademark of Oxford University Press

Library of Congress Cataloging-in-Publication Data
Cunha, Euclides da, 1866–1909.
[A margem da história. English. Selections]
The Amazon : land without history / by Euclides da Cunha; translated from the
Portuguese by Ronald Sousa; edited with an introduction and notes by Lúcia Sá.
p. cm. — (The library of Latin America)
Includes bibliographical references.
ISBN-13: 978-0-19-517204-1 (pbk.)
ISBN-10: 0-19-517204-3 (pbk.)
ISBN-13: 978-0-19-517205-8
ISBN-10: 0-19-517205-1
1. Amazon River Valley—Description and travel.
2. Amazon River Valley—History.
3. Acre (Brazil)—Description and travel.
4. Purus River (Peru and Brazil)—Description and travel.
5. Acre (Brazil)—History.
I. Sousa, Ronald.
II. Sá, Lúcia.
III. Title
IV. Series.
F2546.C938 2006
918.1′1045—dc22
2005035861

1 3 5 7 9 8 6 4 2

Printed in the United States of America
on acid-free paper

Contents

Series Editors'
General Introduction

The Library of Latin America series makes available in translation major nineteenth-century authors whose work has been neglected in the English-speaking world. The titles for the translations from the Spanish and Portuguese were suggested by an editorial committee that included Jean Franco (general editor responsible for works in Spanish), Richard Graham (series editor responsible for works in Portuguese), Tulio Halperín Donghi (University of California–Berkeley), Iván Jaksić (University of Notre Dame), Naomi Lindstrom (University of Texas–Austin), Francine Masiello (University of California–Berkeley), and Eduardo Lozano of the Library at the University of Pittsburgh. The late Antonio Cornejo Polar of the University of California–Berkeley was also one of the founding members of the committee. The translations have been funded thanks to the generosity of the Lampadia Foundation and the Andrew W. Mellon Foundation.

During the period of national formation between 1810 and into the early years of the twentieth century, the new nations of Latin America fashioned their identities, drew up constitutions, engaged in bitter struggles over territory, and debated questions of education, government, ethnicity, and culture. This was a unique period unlike the process of nation formation in Europe and one that should be more familiar than it is to students of comparative politics, history, and literature.

The image of the nation was envisioned by the lettered classes—a minority in countries in which indigenous, mestizo, black or mulatto peasants, and slaves predominated—although alternative nationalisms existed at the grassroots level. The cultural elites were well educated in European thought and letters, but as statesmen, journalists, poets, and academics, they confronted the problem of the racial and linguistic heterogeneity of the continent and the difficulties of integrating the population into a modern nation-state. Some of the writers whose works will be translated in the Library of Latin America series played leading roles in politics. Fray Servando Teresa de Mier, a friar who translated Rousseau's *The Social Contract* and was one of the most colorful characters of the independence period, was faced with imprisonment and expulsion from Mexico for his heterodox beliefs. When he returned after independence, he was elected to the congress. Domingo Faustino Sarmiento, exiled from his native Argentina under the dictatorship of Juan Manuel de Rosas, wrote *Facundo: Civilización y barbarie*, a stinging denunciation of that government. He returned after Rosas's overthrow and was elected president in 1868. Andrés Bello was born in Venezuela, lived in London where he published poetry during the independence period, settled in Chile where he founded the university, wrote a grammar of the Spanish language, and drew up the country's legal code.

This postindependence intelligentsia, far from simply dreaming of castles in the air, vitally contributed to the founding of nations and the shaping of culture. The advantage of hindsight may make us aware of problems they did not foresee, but this should not affect our assessment of their astonishing energy and achievements. Although there is a recent translation of Sarmiento's celebrated *Facundo*, there is no translation of his memoirs, *Recuerdos de provincia* (Provincial Recollections). The predominance of memoirs in the Library of Latin America series is no accident—many offer entertaining insights into a vast, complex continent.

Nor have we neglected the novel. The series includes new translations of the outstanding Brazilian writer Machado de Assis's work, including *Dom Casmurro* and *The Posthumous Memoirs of Brás Cubas*. There is no reason why other novels and writers who are not so well known outside Latin America—the Peruvian novelist Clorinda Matto de Turner's *Aves sin nido*, Nataniel Aguirre's *Juan de la Rosa*, José de Alencar's *Iracema*, Juana Manuela Gorriti's short stories—should not be read with as much interest as the political novels of Anthony Trollope.

However, a series on nineteenth-century Latin America cannot be limited to literary genres such as the novel, the poem, and the short story. The literature of independent Latin America was eclectic and strongly influenced by the periodical press newly liberated from scrutiny by colonial authorities and the Inquisition. Newspapers were miscellanies of fiction, essays, poems, and translations from all manner of European writing. The novels written on the eve of Mexican independence by José Joaquín Fernández de Lizardi included disquisitions on secular education and law, as well as denunciations of the evils of gaming and idleness. Other works, such as a well-known poem by Andrés Bello, "Ode to Tropical Agriculture," and novels such as *Amalia* by José Mármol and the Bolivian Nataniel Aguirre's *Juan de la Rosa* were openly partisan. By the end of the century, sophisticated scholars were beginning to address the history of their countries, as did João Capistrano de Abreu in his *Capítulos de história colonial.*

Memoirs such as those by Fray Servando Teresa de Mier or Sarmiento frequently offer the descriptions of everyday life that in Europe were incorporated into the realist novel. Latin American literature at this time was seen largely as a pedagogical tool, a "light" alternative to speeches, sermons, and philosophical tracts. Especially in the early part of the century, the readership for novels was small because of the high illiteracy rate. Nevertheless, the orally transmitted culture of the gaucho and the urban underclasses became the linguistic repertoire of some of the most interesting nineteenth-century writers—notably José Hernández, author of the "gauchesque" poem "Martín Fierro," which enjoyed an unparalleled popularity. For many writers the task was not to appropriate popular language but to civilize, and their literary works were strongly influenced by the high style of political oratory.

The editorial committee has not attempted to limit its selection to the better-known writers such as Machado de Assis; it has also selected many works that have never appeared in translation or writers whose works have not been translated recently. The series now makes these works available to the English-speaking public.

Because of the preferences of funding organizations, the series initially focuses on writing from Brazil, the Southern Cone, the Andean region, and Mexico. Each of our editions will have an introduction that places the work in its appropriate context and includes explanatory notes.

We owe special thanks to the late Robert Glynn of the Lampadia Foundation, whose initiative jump-started the project, and Richard Ekman and his successors at the Andrew W. Mellon Foundation, which generously supported the project. We also thank the Rockefeller Foundation for funding the 1996 symposium, Culture and Nation in Iberoamerica, organized by the editorial board of the Library of Latin America. The support of Edward Barry of Oxford University Press was crucial in the founding years of the project, as was the assistance of Ellen Chodosh and Elda Rotor of Oxford University Press. The John Carter Brown Library at Brown University in Providence, Rhode Island, has served as the grant administrator of the project since 1998.

—Jean Franco
—Richard Graham

Introduction
Voicing Brazilian Imperialism:
Euclides da Cunha and the Amazon

The essays included in *Land Without History* are the result of a long trip Euclides da Cunha made to the Amazon in 1905 as a member of a joint Brazil–Peru expedition to determine the borders between the two nations. This trip had a profound impact on Euclides,[1] who became obsessed with the idea of writing a long book on the region entitled *Lost Paradise*, which would do for the Amazon what his celebrated *Os sertões*[2] did for the northeastern *sertão*: introduce the educated urban populations of the south to tropical backlands of Brazil they knew little about. However, Euclides never completed this project. He produced instead a series of separate essays, most of which (the ones translated here) he later turned into the first part of the book *À margem da história*, published soon after his tragic death in 1909.[3]

What gives these texts their edge is in part the cultlike status their author enjoys in Brazilian intellectual history. Even though Brazil has produced several writers more important than Euclides, few (if any) have been so prominently featured in exhibitions, special conferences, political and academic discourse. Not only has the cabin where he wrote *Os sertões* been preserved as an object of cultural pilgrimage, but it has also been covered with a protective structure resembling a shrine. He is revered by critics on the right and the left as a writer who penetrated the soul of his nation as no other before or after him. Yet commentaries on his most important book, *Os sertões*, have from the start been hedged by justification and excuse. Critics say that he sometimes adhered too closely to positivist models of science and knowledge, but he also was able to subvert and contradict such models.[4] His style—a disconcerting mixture of the scientific jargon of the day and hyperbolic literary image (imitated by minor writers for decades after his death)—verges on bad taste, though, as critics are also quick to observe, it never quite crosses that line.[5] Dramatic events in his biography have also helped feed the Euclides da Cunha myth: in 1909 he was killed by his wife's young lover, as was his son, years later, when attempting to avenge his father's death.

Of course Euclides's writing style and personal life are not enough to explain the fascination he exerts in Brazil and beyond. Perhaps the main reason for such fascination is Euclides's problematic self-location within his own texts, which resembles, one might add, the position sustained today by many Brazilian intellectuals with regard to the poor and un-educated masses of the country. This problematic position makes the essays in *Land Without History* an important landmark in Latin American writing. They hardly provide us with a thorough or detailed account of the Amazon in the early twentieth century. Rather, what these essays offer us is a compelling testimony to the Brazilian colonial enterprise in the Amazon, and to its imperialist tendencies with regard to neigh-boring nation-states.

In order to understand Euclides's position in these Amazonian essays we have to take a brief look at the text that made him famous overnight: *Os sertões*. Published in 1902, it is an account of how a community of supposed monarchists in the backlands of Bahia was repressed by republican Brazil. Euclides, who was an engineer by formation, went to the site of Canudos as a reporter for the newspaper *O Estado de São Paulo*. He had already published an article about the monarchist revolt in the same paper, entitled "A nossa vendéia" (Our Vendée)—effectively incorporating Canudos into the European scheme of the French Revolution. The Canudos rebellion was in the news constantly at the time: headlines fed the panic of urban readers by exaggerating the size of the revolt and its political significance as an antirepublican movement. Euclides wrote *Os sertões* immediately after returning from the field. The opinions expressed in the book differ considerably from the Vendée art-icle: the monarchist motivation is replaced with a portrait of the *sertanejos* that oscillates between deploring them as confused religious fanatics and sympathizing with them as poverty-ridden *mestiços* left out of the newly created republican dream. The latter position made *Os sertões* an enlightening study of Brazilian society that allowed literate urban Brazilians, especially southerners, to contemplate another Brazil inland and far north: a Brazil that was not—and did not want to be—part of the elites' modernizing project. Elected to the Brazilian Literary Academy just one year after publishing *Os sertões*, Euclides da Cunha became one of Brazil's most celebrated writers, even though his book could scarcely be classified as "literature" in any conventional way. As critics have repeatedly pointed out, *Os sertões* mixes several genres: "scientific" report, sociology, history, military record, journalism, and poetic prose. What makes it extraordinary is the author/narrator's oscillation, the "scientific" prejudices he embraces against the "backward *sertanejos*" and his perplexed admiration of their capacity to resist; his enduring support of the military campaign and his denunciations of it as a brutal massacre.

Euclides's position with regard to the Canudos massacre expresses what Renato Rosaldo refers to as "a particular kind of nostalgia, often found under imperialism, where people mourn the passing of what they themselves have transformed" (69). This "imperialist nostalgia," an unavoidable element in colonial enterprises, is also seen in the trajectory of ethnographers who unwittingly contribute to the destruction of the very cultures they devote themselves to. A project of and for the elites, the Brazilian nation at independence incorporated by force several groups that had no wish to be part of it; revolts in different parts of the country—like the Cabanagem in Pará and the Farroupilha in the south—had already demonstrated that national unity was by no means guaranteed. Canudos was the last of these major regional revolts, and a particularly remarkable one for the southern elites because it was apparently sparked by the declaration of the federal republic. The Brazilian state assault on Canudos is in that sense a colonialist enterprise: an attempt to forcibly dominate a group that it saw as unwilling to join the national project. As an "embedded" journalist accompanying the last of the military expeditions and a former army man himself, Euclides devotes dozens of pages of his long book to describing, with undeniable fascination, the war and its strategies. At the same time, his growing admiration for what he calls the "backward *sertanejos*" leads him to risk modifying scientific theory of the time to explain how, racially mixed as they may have been, the *sertanejos* were well adapted to their environment—a rare case of an "inferior race" (the Indian) that nonetheless had prevailed. In spite of his praise for the bravery and resilience of the *sertanejo*, and in spite of his final condemnation of the military invasion, Euclides had participated in the destruction of Canudos. Not only that, he also belonged to and identified himself with the urban elites who took it upon themselves to civilize, by force, the rest of the country. There can be no better expression of imperial nostalgia than his famous sentence from *Rebellion*, "We are condemned to civilization" (54). The paradox of his formulation is perfectly congruent with Rosaldo's definition of imperialist nostalgia: "Imperialist nostalgia revolves around a paradox: A person kills somebody, and then mourns the victim. In more attenuated form, someone deliberately alters a form of life, and then regrets that things have not remained as they were prior to the intervention" (68–69).

As Euclides moved from *Rebellion in the Backlands* to the Amazonian essays, his imperialist nostalgia seemed to give way, almost entirely, to straightforward imperialism: instead of blaming himself or his own country for eliminating cultures and the environment, he blamed other countries or the victims themselves. Yet the paradox that defines imperialist nostalgia is still present in these essays in the way Euclides uses the *sertanejos* to condemn and promote Brazil's activities and involvement in the Amazon.

Euclides went to the Amazon heading the Brazilian party in the binational border expedition, and as such he was inevitably compromised by his country's official position with regard to the region. Less than two years before his journey, Brazil and Bolivia had signed the Petrópolis Treaty of 1903, with Bolivia ceding to Brazil her undeniable rights (according to international law) to a great proportion of Acre in exchange for 2 million pounds sterling and the perpetual right of free transit on the Amazonian system in Brazil. For its part, Brazil took on the border questions between Bolivia and Peru. Many Brazilians and most of Brazil's neighbors saw the treaty as a heavy-handed diplomatic intervention backed by unreasonable military threats.[6] The treaty consolidated the Brazilian imperialist position in the Amazon and, to a certain degree, in the rest of South America. It resulted from several years of bitter negotiations between the two nations, which included two revolutions in Acre (one of which won it a temporary independent status as the Republic of Acre), several military battles with many deaths on both sides, and an array of diplomatic exchanges not only between Brazil and Bolivia, but also between these two nations and the United States (which was accused, in the aftermath of 1898, of trying to take control of the region), Peru, Great Britain, Chile, and Argentina. The main argument used at the time by those who defended Brazil's right to Acre was the concept of *uti possidetis*—the idea that the territory should belong to those who occupy it productively. In those years Acre was economically important because of its large production of rubber, an extremely valuable commodity in international trade. This production attracted immense numbers of migrant workers from the drought-ridden region of Ceará in the *sertão*. The *cearenses* occupied a sizable part of the territory that belonged legally to Bolivia, and when the Bolivians tried to assert fiscal control over it, the newcomers initiated a revolt backed in part by the large rubber companies of Manaus.

Less than two years after the treaty was signed, Euclides traveled to Acre with the responsibility of settling the borders between Brazil's newly acquired territory and Peru. It was a tense trip, full of nationalistic bravado, that ended unsatisfactorily for both sides.[7] Euclides's view of the Amazon is thus colored by his official position and will seem most unfamiliar to contemporary readers. Images nowadays associated with the world's largest rain forest—the diversity of the fauna and flora, the presence of indigenous populations, traditions of native and local knowledge—are conspicuously absent. Instead, the Amazon is presented in *Land Without History* as a new land whose function and destiny is to be colonized.

Like *Os sertões*, this collection of essays begins with a physical description of the territory that mixes scientific jargon with passionate and highly personal views. The aim of such descriptions is, in both books, to establish a topographic grounding for the arguments that the author goes on to develop. *Os sertões*, for instance, presents the plants and land of the *sertão* as resilient and strong, capable of enduring the worst hardship— a description that prefigures that of the *sertanejos* themselves later on in the book. In *Land Without History*, the first essay describes nature as incomplete, imperfect, unfinished. The great rivers, especially the Amazon, are said to be always destroying their own banks and spreading into new beds elsewhere. The only type of human adaptation that has worked in the region is, according to Euclides, nomadic, because nature is inconstant and eliminates, through self-destruction, all traces of its own history. By presenting Amazonian nature this way, Euclides makes land practically nonexistent as a physical concept, replacing it with territorial definitions based on human action. In describing physical borders as inherently unstable, Euclides prepares the way for the later essays in the book, when he gives the *sertanejo* settlers full credit for the territorial definition of Acre: "But they [the *sertanejos*] did not disappear. On the contrary, in less than thirty years the area that was a vague geographical term, a swampy wilderness stretching out limitlessly to the southwest, has suddenly defined itself, contributing substantially to our economic development" (57). In other words, borders can stabilize only after the Brazilian workers arrive and found towns and villages. The spatial logic of the Amazon here, for Euclides, is the logic of *uti possidetis*.

It is not only land that is denied physical stability in this essay. As the title of the book tells us, history is also marginal or nonexistent in the Amazonian region. When describing the Amazon River, for instance, Euclides claims that the banks seen in the sixteenth-century by Francisco Orellana, the first European to sail down it, have been destroyed by the river itself—history, in other words, has been washed away physically. This reference becomes even more significant when we recall Fray Gaspar de Carvajal's account of Orellana's expedition, which describes the banks of the Amazon as being massively populated by native peoples. The fact that Carvajal's accounts are now being corroborated by the archaeological excavations led by Anna Roosevelt seriously weakens Euclides's arguments, for no excavation would be possible had the river banks been destroyed as definitively as he claimed. Euclides's destruction of the banks of the Amazon River in the first of his Amazonian essays is a way of eliminating all history prior to the arrival of the Europeans in the region, and therefore any possible land claims by the only truly legitimate owners of the Amazon, the original native American inhabitants. This helps us understand why native Americans are mostly absent in *Land Without History*, and overwhelmingly so in the first essays in the book, precisely those essays that define the region historically and geographically. The first essay, for instance, mentions native peoples only in passing, as part of a discourse that highlights how most attempts to bring "progress" to the region had failed. For the most part, after reading the first three essays in the book one could be forgiven for believing that Acre was originally an empty territory that became populated only after the arrival of the *cearenses*. This is the case, for instance, in Euclides's reference to the area having been occupied for "three centuries" (14)—an explicit denial of human life in the Amazon prior to the Europeans; or in his comments on Amazonian landscape as inimical to human occupation: "The topographic forms most associated with human existence are absent. There is something unearthly about this amphibian nature, this mixture of land and water" (32). Such references contradict awareness of prior and present occupation in the Amazon generally and in Acre specifically, which he shows elsewhere in his book, as well as an established bibliography about the Amazon that he must have been well acquainted with: Couto de Magalhães's *O selvagem* (1876), Barbosa Rodrigues's *Poranduba amazonense* (1890), and Ermanno Stradelli's *Jurupari* (1890), for instance, all of which affirm the primary significance not just of native occupation of the region but of native accounts of that occupation.

The first appearance of live indigenous people in *Land Without History* is quite curious and comes only at the end of the third essay, "This Accursed Climate." Among the foreigners (non-Brazilians) who have been settling in the Purus region, Euclides includes the "adventurous, artistic Italian who spends long months traveling the rivers with photographic equipment collecting the most typical faces of the Indians in the forest and scenes of the wild countryside" (42). For the first time the reader is made aware of the present existence of indigenous peoples in the region, but even so they are phantasmagoric, captured in the "wild" through the lenses of an "artistic" European traveler.

In the fourth essay, "The Caucheros," Euclides ingeniously distinguishes the Indians he meets on Brazilian territory from those who appear on the Peruvian side. To begin with, Brazilian Indians are mentioned, once again, only in passing, in order to be contrasted with the truly dangerous peoples that inhabit the Peruvian lands of Madre de Dios:

> Anyone going up the Purus and observing, in the area around Cachoeira, the Paumaris, ever decreasing in number and hardly recalling the old masters of those lands, or further upstream, the peaceful Ipurinás, or even past the Yaco, the Tacunas, born looking old, so much is the decrepitude of their race reflected in their stunted aspect, will be surprised when he comes face-to-face with the singular savages who populate the [Peruvian] headwaters. (45)

If the adjectives used to refer to Brazilian Indians describe them as creatures on their way to extinction or docile observers of the colonization of the region, the description of the natives on the Peruvian side is quite different in tone:

> The bronzed Piros, with shiny teeth stained with a dark resin that give their faces an indefinable aspect of grave threat when they smile. The bearded Caxibos, inured to extermination after two hundred years of attacks against the remains of the Pachitea missions. The Conibos, with deformed craniums and chests frighteningly striped red and blue. The Setebos, the Sipibos, the Iurimanas. The corpulent Maschcos of the Manú, recalling in their great size the giants imagined by the first cartographers of the Amazon region. And above all others, supplanting them in valor and renown, the warlike Campas of the Urubamba. (45)

While the Brazilian Indians, as Euclides describes them, do not pose any present threat to his country's economic exploitation of the region, the natives on the Peruvian side elicit fear. Although Brazil has achieved the domination of its own territory, Peru has yet to "conquer the savages," has as yet no rightful control over the territory it wants to claim. In a halfhearted attempt at imperialist nostalgia, Euclides then laments the destruction of the Indians, and this time includes Brazilian and Bolivian settlers among the aggressors: "Civilization, barbarously armed with its lethal rifles, completely besieges here the cornered savage. The Peruvians from the west and from the south; the Brazilians in the entire northeastern sector; and on the southeast the Bolivians, shutting off access to the Madre de Dios Valley" (46). But it is the Peruvian *caucheros*, according to him, who are most responsible for the present extermination: "And the *caucheros* appear as the most advantaged intruders in this sinister catechism of fire and sword that, off in this remote backland, continues to exterminate the most interesting native peoples of South America" (70). The uncharacteristic weakness and vagueness of the adjective ("interesting") used to describe the native peoples who are being exterminated signals how unconvincing the author's nostalgia actually is—and this is mostly because he can blame the present killing on the Peruvians. In the same essay, he describes how the binational expedition encountered an ailing native abandoned by the Peruvian *caucheros*: "In one of the better preserved of the outlying buildings, the last inhabitant awaited us. Piro, Amauaca, or Campa, his provenience was indistinguishable. His repulsive appearance transformed the very features of the human species: a huge trunk bloated with malaria dominated, in obvious contrast to thin arms and thin, withered legs, like those of a monstrous fetus" (55). Though referring here to someone left behind in an abandoned *caucho* extraction complex, "last inhabitant" can also be read, in line with a popular literary trope of the time, as the last representative of a race that has been exterminated. In most of its literary appearances, the concept of the "last inhabitant" is tied to sentimental imperialist nostalgia, and it betrays a degree of wishful thinking, for seldom is the "inhabitant" actually the last one. In Euclides's case, the poignancy of the scene suggests imperialist nostalgia, as we are meant to feel pity for the poor Indian who is being killed by our own "civilization." But not for long; once again, Euclides points to the "true cause" of the Indian's demise, the Peruvian *caucheros*: "opening up with rifle balls and machete strokes new paths for their frenetic coming and going, and revealing other unknown areas, where they would leave behind, as they had here, in the fallen-in buildings or the pitiful figure of the sacrificed Indian, the only fruits of their tumultuous undertaking, fruits of their role as builders of ruins" (55). The *caucheros* are "builders of ruins" because, unlike the Brazilian *sertanejos*, they do not settle in a permanent place. Again, the logic of *uti possidetis* permeates the essay: Brazil has acquired the right to Acre through the activities of its *sertanejo* settlers. Peru, on the other hand, is still fighting its Indians, and through men (the *caucheros*) who cannot settle or build anything, just destroy.

This is probably the main argument in *Land Without History*, and Euclides makes it again and again. In "Brazilians" he claims that the colonization of what is now the Peruvian Amazon was actually achieved by Brazilians. It was a Brazilian, according to him, who "discovered *caucho* or, at least, established the industry of its extraction" (70). In 1841 a Brazilian was given exclusive license to run a steam fleet to carry goods from eastern Peru down the Amazon River. And finally, Brazilian *sertanejos* were responsible for the only successful settlements in the Peruvian Amazon—which fell into ruin once these Brazilians were forced out. Incidentally, the activities of *sertanejos* in Peru included killing Indians, but since this happened in the past as part of attempts to settle the region, the killings are described as a heroic struggle against peoples such as the Caxibos, the "wildest of the tribes of the Ucayali Valley" (74).

In making these claims, Euclides never explicitly states that Brazil should demand rights to parts of the Peruvian Amazon. Rather, he tries to legitimize what was, by most accounts, Brazil's dubious claim to Acre.

He also wants to affirm Brazil's superior position with regard to its neighbors. That his discourse was imperialist (with regard to other South American nations) and colonialist (with regard to Amazonia, which, according to him, should be "civilized" by Brazil) becomes even clearer in the explicit and frequent comparisons with the English and French colonial enterprises in India and Africa. And in the last essay in this collection he makes a plea for the construction of a railway linking Cruzeiro do Sul to Acre because, besides the obvious economic reasons, it would allow Brazil to defend its territory in case of war.

Euclides's hero in the Brazilian colonization of the Amazon is the *sertanejo*, the migrant worker who fled the drought-ridden Ceará. In this sense *Land Without History* is a continuation of *Os sertões*: the strong and brave *sertanejos* who ended the first book under attack from the Brazilian army reappear now in Acre, expanding Brazilian frontiers. As in the first book, the *sertanejo* of *Land Without History* is an unlikely hero who is described in contradictory terms. On the one hand he is the protagonist of what Euclides calls "haphazard colonization" (*colonização à gandaia*), an unplanned and disorganized process of colonization that produced better results than the well-planned enterprises of Britain in India or France in Indochina. Poor, ailing, with no help from the Brazilian state, the *sertanejo*, according to Euclides, went to the Amazon and killed Indians, founded towns, started the economic development of the region, conquered Acre, and stimulated the "civilizing" enterprises in the Peruvian territory, as we just saw. On the other hand, the same *sertanejo* is presented as a pathetic figure who sought his own slavery and had no sense of controlling his own destiny.

In the first essay, for instance, Euclides gives a detailed account of the *sertanejo's* economic endurance and the unfairness of the rubber-tapping system that enslaves him. At the end of the essay he makes a strong social claim: "What comes definitively to the fore, however, is the urgent need of measures to rescue this hidden and abandoned culture: a work law that would ennoble human effort; an austere justice that would curb excesses; and some form of homestead provision that would definitively link man and the land" (17). Powerful and clear as they are, the provisions Euclides demanded would require nothing less than a revolution, and have yet to be implemented. It is not obvious how the *sertanejo's* lack of perspective can become, in other passages, a strong agency and capacity to make his own history, since he is a "portentous anomaly: he is the man who toils in order to enslave himself" (14). The problem is not so much Euclides's description of rubber tapping as an unjust economic system, as "the most heinous organization of labor ever conjured up by human egotism unbound" (14)—which is basically true—but his simultaneous celebration of that system as crucial to the Brazilian economy and as a guarantee of power over Brazil's neighbors. This contradiction is at the core of his Amazonian essays, and, as with *Os sertões*, is probably what makes these texts so compelling. As an unlikely hero, the *sertanejo* is fit to represent Brazil as the unlikely modern nation. In other words, the *sertanejo* is a hero in spite of his mixed race (a clear problem for Euclides, who believed in the scientific precepts of his time), his lack of education, his poor health, and the unjust economic system that does not help him—precisely the conditions that many national and international analysts of the time thought would keep Brazil from entering modernity.

"Judas Ahasverus," which most critics consider the best text in this collection and the most rounded of Euclides's writings, is a good example of how these contradictions play out.[8] Centered on the common folkloric festivity of beating Judas, which happens throughout Brazil the Saturday before Easter Sunday, Euclides discusses the special local characteristics it acquired in Amazonia, among the *sertanejo* rubber tappers. Instead of an unspecific straw doll, in Amazonia Judas is made, according to Euclides, to resemble the rubber tapper (*seringueiro*) himself. The doll is then placed in a small boat that is sent down river, and the *seringueiros* shoot at it as it passes by. For Euclides, this particular manifestation of Judas beating is an expression of self-hatred:

> It is a dolorous triumph. The *sertanejo* has sculpted the accursed figure in his own image. He has taken revenge on himself. In the final analysis he has punished himself for the accursed ambition that brought him to this land and takes revenge on himself for the moral weakness that shatters his impulse to rebel, pushing it even further onto the lower plane of this degenerate life where infantile credulity has tied him to this swampy realm controlled by scoundrels who deceive him (60).

"Judas Ahasverus" comes close to being poetic prose, if at times a little too precious. At the same time, it maintains the analytical voice that marks all of Euclides's essays. Clearly the narrator sees the *sertanejo* rubber tapper as an object of study with no voice of his own; a large part of the essay describes the Judas doll going down river as if he were the rubber tapper. In that role, the *sertanejo* hardly resembles the hero of Amazonian colonization described by Euclides elsewhere in these essays. Melancholy, tied to a brutal system he cannot escape, the *sertanejo* in "Judas Ahasverus" can only resort to his yearly festival of self-hatred. But if we look beyond Euclides's seductive construction of the *sertanejo* doll man, we will see that his whole argument rests on the care that the *sertanejo* puts into making the doll, even giving it his own hat. On the other hand, both facts are common to the custom of making Judas dolls all over Brazil, and not necessarily synonymous with self-hatred (after all, what hat would the *sertanejo* give the doll other then his own?). Because the *sertanejo* is never given a voice, we can never hear about the fun that he and his children must find in those festivities, even less about the sense of community implicit in the fact that all *seringueiros* recognize the Judas dolls that pass by as objects of play in a shared game.

Euclides's Judas may be the object of the *seringueiro*'s self-hatred, but it could also represent the boat salesmen who travel up and down river, the owners of the *seringais*, or indeed the biblical Judas. And even if Euclides's description of the festivity as an expression of self-hatred, what would be the cause of that self-hatred if not the colonization of the Amazon that Euclides urges and celebrates? By choosing to describe the *seringueiros*'s Judas beating as self-hatred, Euclides blames the victims of a colonization process that he is helping promote. Imperial nostalgia is therefore transferred to the weaker perpetrators of the colonizing process, victims of an unjust economic system that is the heart and staple of all colonizing enterprises in the world.

The essays in *Land Without History* open a rare window onto the process of consolidation of the South American nation-states. At a time when rubber was one of the most desired commodities in the world, the Amazon naturally occupied a central role in this process. Euclides's peculiar mixture of strong literary imagery and positivist scientific argumentation (brilliantly translated into Victorian English by Ronald Sousa) brings us into the heart of early twentieth-century Latin American thought. If "scientific truths" were made to serve the interest of the racist and colonialist elites, poetry, on the other hand, offered sentimental compensation and compassion. Imperialist nostalgia helped define, in other words, Euclides's famously idiosyncratic style. Brazilian colonialism and imperialism have never since found expression in a voice more eloquent and talented than his.

NOTES

1. In Brazilian cultural history and criticism, the author is generally referred to as Euclides.

2. *Os sertões* has a magnificent translation by Samuel Putnam entitled *Rebellion in the Backlands*. I refer to the original title to maintain the specificity of the place *sertão*, which means not "backlands" in general but a particular area in the northeastern interior often plagued by drought. People from the *sertão*, the *sertanejos*, are an important presence in *Land Without History*, as we will see.

3. A few other essays Euclides wrote about the Amazon are included in, for example, *Relatório da comissão mista brasileiro-peruana de reconhecimento do alto purus* (1906), *Contrastes e confrontos* (1907), and *Peru versus Bolívia* (1907). I chose to include only the essays from *À margem da história* because they were put together as a unit by the author. A compilation that included all of his Amazonian texts would include considerable repetition and some highly technical texts. Such a compilation was made, in Portuguese, by Heldon Rocha, entitled *Um paraíso perdido: Reunião dos ensaios amazônicos* (1976). For an excellent analysis of Euclides's Amazonian essays, see Hardman.

4. See, for instance, Alfredo Bosi, *História concisa da literatura brasileira* (São Paulo: Cultrix, 1970); and Luiz Costa Lima, "Os Sertões: Ciência ou literatura?" *Revista Tempo Brasileiro* 144 (2001).

5. See Gilberto Freyre, "Euclides da Cunha: Revelador da realidade brasileira," in Euclides da Cunha, *Obra completa* (Rio: Aguilar, 1966), 1:17–31.

6. See Charles Stokes, "The Acre Revolutions, 1899–1903: A Study in Brazilian Expansionism" (Ph.D. diss., Tulane University, 1974).

7. See *Relatório da comissão mista* and Tocantins.

8. See, for instance, Márcio José Lauria, "Judas-Ahsverus," in *Enciclopédia de estudos euclidianos*, vol. 1 (Jundiaí: Jundiá, 1982).

Translator's Note

If ever a text challenged the notion that translation can be a systematic undertaking, this collection of seven short essays by the Brazilian writer Euclides da Cunha constitutes such a text. It includes a mixture of multiple discourses, including public policy, the discourses of several fields of applied science including multiple branches of engineering, and a rhetoric with paragraph-long sentences that at times seems fetched directly from the seventeenth century. *The Amazon: Land Without History* virtually imposes a translation strategy grounded in practical goals and tactical-decision making rather than any overall theory. In translating, I found myself making a choice that I felt appropriate for the specific passage on which I was working but contradicted the logic of choices made elsewhere in the text using the same criterion of appropriateness. As a result, I find it incumbent on myself to advise the reader of some of the practical goals I set and the tactics I used to carry them out.

First and foremost, I sought to render the basic content of the original and, second, to present it in a form as much like the original as possible. While those twin goals may seem straightforward and mutually compatible—and susceptible to overall theorization—the contrary is in fact the case. The first goal is made complex by the fact that English is unable to render the subordinate-clause-within-subordinate-clause structure that Portuguese can sustain (albeit with much strain). Euclides da Cunha is capable of introducing a subordinate clause or even an adjective that initiates a line of argument digressive from, and sometimes even contradictory to, the main argument of the sentence in which it appears. Consequently while I try, sometimes to the point of producing tortured English, to reproduce wherever I can the overall lineaments of the author's argument and something of his manner of presenting that argument—long subordinate structures, strings of adjectives or adjectival phrases—more often than not I find myself limited to mere recapitulation of the general import in sentences quite unlike his. (The editor, Lúcia Sá, generously refers to the result as "Victorian English." Would that it had that degree of consistency!) At times I am constrained to recapture parts of the original argument by means and in locations quite different from those of the target text. In short, much as Putnam did in his celebrated rendering of *Os sertões* (*Rebellion in the Backlands*, 1944), I engage in what at times is almost a "writing about" Euclides da Cunha's texts. Given the great difference between the two originals, however, this "writing about" is quite different from Putnam's—and I fear much less cohesive.

The second of my goals seeks to compensate for the way I carry out the first. With a few exceptions having to do with what is acceptable in current English prose writing, I faithfully reproduce the highly idiosyncratic paragraphing and section divisions of the original. In the English, then, the reader will be able to follow the author's overall argumentative sequence, even though the specific argumentation within that sequence will vary considerably from that of the original.

I have consulted two editions of the original to create my target text: *À margem da história* ([São Paulo]: Editora Lello Brasileira, 1967), and *Um paraíso perdido: Reunião dos ensaios amazônicos* (Petrópolis: Editora Vozes, 1976). Unfortunately they do not always agree in their readings. One sometimes functions as corrective for an obviously corrupt reading in the other. On this point, I have simply followed the logic of coherence rather than taking either text as master. On the issue of paragraphing and section division, which also varies between the two, I have followed *À margem da história*.

Two of the essays, "Rivers in Abandon" and "Brazilians," were published by the author in Brazilian periodicals. Internal evidence—which does not show through in my translation—suggests that the latter was edited from a longer version. I have no idea about the current status of that longer version.

My goals in translating have been challenged in other ways as well. While written in Portuguese, the original contains extended passages in English and Spanish as well as phrases in French, German, Latin, and Italian, and mentions in several Amerindian languages rendered in Portuguese. I have found it impossible to simultaneously maintain a sense that the reader is being presented an English version of Euclides da Cunha's original and signal in any consistent way the presence of those other languages in the text. To attempt that task would have required either intrusive editorial parentheses or extensive footnotes, neither of which would have contributed to realization of my second goal. The latter measure, moreover, would have competed with the footnotes that are one dimension of the original. Consequently the reader must understand that at times she or he may be reading, for example, English that is the direct presentation of an English original; however, there is no way to know for certain without consulting the original text. Since the author is not always scrupulous in attribution, the English may be a translation from a Portuguese translation of an English original that was not given citation and I was unable to track down.

Conversely, when I find it tactically effective and the meaning generally clear, I leave short phrases in the original language, since that practice is allowed in current English expository writing and imparts a sense of the texture of the original.

The presence of Spanish in the text deserves mention. Especially in "The Caucheros" and "Brazilians," whose very subject matter centrally involves the interpenetration of Spanish- and Portuguese-language cultures in Amazonia, a great deal of Spanish appears—or sometimes merely what Euclides da Cunha thinks the Spanish should be based on his Portuguese. Since some of that Spanish has to do with terminology attendant on the issues being presented, I have attempted to set up Spanish-language terms, lightly glossed in context so the meaning is made clear, for repeated use. Also, when the same word is written differently in Spanish and Portuguese, I settle on one or the other according to my sense of the focus of the text. For instance, I use the Spanish form "Ucayali" to refer to the river that Euclides da Cunha names "Ucaiali" because references to it in his text have to do with Peruvian terrain more than with Brazilian.

The practice of setting up terms for reuse with a light contextual glossing on first mention is not limited to Spanish. I use it with Portuguese terms as well—following Euclides da Cunha's own practice for the benefit of his own, principally southern Brazilian readership. My glosses, which are at times decidedly more intrusive than the author's, represent the only additions I make to the text proper. The editor's appended glossary provides general definition of repeated and important terms.

As for the footnotes, in concert with the second of my goals in translating, the reader can be assured that they all come from the original and are faithfully reproduced. I have, however, improved the bibliographical information in them in those places where I could. The improvements in the footnotes represent the only other addition on my part to the original text.

The footnotes present a curious inverse problem in that the author alludes to many works that he does not footnote. Some of those works are one-time mentions and the reader, should he or she wish, can ferret them out. I leave those as they are in the original. Let me give a short list of titles that clarify what I consider important or repeated references that go undocumented in the original.

First, several references early in the original to the work of "Wallace" are made to Alfred Russel Wallace, *A Narrative of Travels on the Amazon and Rio Negro* (London: 1853). The title was multiply reedited.

Second, Alexandre Rodrigues Ferreira's "philosophical voyage" refers to the writing of the explorer by that name who in the 1780s and early 1790s made a number of trips through Amazonia. His writings about those trips, which include literally hundreds of companion drawings, were generally entitled "Viagem filosófica pelas capitanias do Grão Pará, Rio Negro, Mato Grosso e Cuiabá" (Philosophical Voyage through the Captaincies of Grão Pará, Rio Negro, Mato Grosso, and Cuiabá).

Third, despite the author's assertion in the second essay, William Morris Davis, "The Rivers and Valleys of Pennsylvania," which he does not document, was not a book but rather an article in the *National Geographic* 1, no. 3 (1889): 183–253. It may, of course, have been extracted and bound after publication.

Fourth, as Lúcia Sá explains in her excellent introduction, Euclides da Cunha was the Brazilian commissioner on the joint Peruvian–Brazilian commission that traveled and mapped the Upper Purus river in 1904 and 1905 to establish information for fixing the boundary between the two countries. The essays in this volume result from that undertaking, and the author reflects his experience in many ways, overt and subtle, in these pages. The Peruvian commission produced a volume of documents about the undertaking. It is *Reconocimiento de los ríos alto purus i alto yuruá* (Lima, 1906). That volume includes a detailed foldout map made by the commission, which can serve as a virtual companion to parts of the second essay in this book. To a lesser extent, the entire volume serves in that relationship to the entirety of what follows. The map bears the coauthorial name "el Ingeniero Brasileño Sr. Euclides da Cunha." The map is done in Spanish and as a consequence presents some place-names that are known today in Portuguese, or by Amerindian names rendered in Portuguese, in Spanish-based forms.

Finally, I offer three notes that I think some readers will find useful. First, the Amerindian group that the author refers to as "Campas" is usually referred to today as the Asháninka. Over the past quarter century a considerable literature has been written about it.

Second, in contrast with Putnam's precedent, I leave the words *sertão* (pl. *sertões*) and *sertanejo* in the original Portuguese in order to point out their geographical specificity: the drought-plagued northeastern interior of Brazil and dwellers in, or refugees from, that region. (See Lúcia Sá's introduction for further development of the role of the *sertão* in these essays.)

Last, the word that I, following others before me, translate as "paths" (the Portuguese is *estradas*) is a key term in the text. Literally it refers to the looping, circular paths that the rubber tapper walked to gather the accumulated raw latex, as well as to the stand of rubber-producing trees assigned to an individual tapper. That number usually ranged in the area of 100 to 130. Euclides da Cunha uses the term metaphorically in a number of different ways to the extent that it comes to characterize early-twentieth-century Amazonian life as he analyzes it. However, it could just as easily characterize the text in which he presents that analysis—in which case this is the starting point from which the reader and I shall set out to walk Euclides da Cunha's "paths."

—RS
2006

The Amazon

General Impressions

Rather than admiration and enthusiasm, what usually comes over someone beholding the Amazon at the point where the Tajapuru's vibrant confusion flows full into the great river is a sense of disillusionment. To be sure, the sheer volume of water is unmatched and therefore capable of inducing that wonderment of which Wallace speaks. But since, from early on in life, each of us has drawn an ideal Amazonia in our minds thanks to the remarkably lyrical pages left us by the countless travelers, from Humboldt down to today, who have contemplated the prodigious hylean rain forest with almost religious awe, we experience a common psychological reaction when we come face to face with the real Amazon: we see it as somehow lacking with respect to the subjective image we have long held of it. Beyond that, as a strictly artistic phenomenon—that is, as a place on earth overflowing with images susceptible of being harmoniously fused into an awe-inspiring synthetic sense—it is decidedly inferior to countless other sites in our own country. In this regard, the entire Amazonian region cannot match, for example, the stretch of our coastline that runs from Cabo Frio to Ponta de Munduba.

It is, nonetheless, doubtless the greatest sight in the land. That sight, however, is one restricted to the horizontal plane, for, much like the last remnants of an enormous, broken frame, the sandstone Monte Alegre range and the granite mountains of the Guianas now rise so little as to provide but a scant touch of relief on one side. And because of this lack of the vertical dimension, essential to imparting a sense of life to a landscape, within a few hours the observer tires in the face of an unbearable monotony and begins to notice that their gaze is less and less frequently directed to that endless horizon as empty and undefined as that of the sea.

The overwhelming impression I conceived—perhaps corresponding to a positive truth—is this: humankind is still an impertinent interloper here. We have arrived uninvited and unprepared for, while nature was still in the process of setting up this vast, magnificent salon. Here we encounter disorder on a lavish scale . . . the rivers are still not fixed in their courses. They seem to search vainly for equilibrium by wandering off aimlessly in unstable meanders that curve into the form of lakes called *sacados* with isthmuses that repeatedly break down and recombine in the futile creation of islands and lakes of only six months' duration. They even produce new topographic forms of jumbled island and lake. Or they extend in cross channels called *furos* that anastomose between the courses of river and tributary in an atypical network fashion, until it is impossible to decide if the area is a river basin or a sea profusely segmented by straits.

A single flood season would completely destroy the work of a hydrographer.

The flora display this same imperfect grandeur. During the silent middays (the nights are fantastically noisy) one who might walk the forest does so with their gaze exhausted by the green-black of the foliage and, repeatedly encountering the arborescent ferns, which rival palm trees in height, and trees with straight, almost bare trunks, does so with the disquieting sense that they have returned to a much earlier time, as though they had invaded the recesses of one of those mute Carboniferous forests the existence of which is known to us through the retrospective gaze of the geologist.

That sensation of extreme antiquity is completed by the set of singular, and monstrous, fauna, where the amphibian dominates by dint of sheer size—all of which adds yet further to the Paleozoic impression. And one who might wander along the rivers not infrequently encounters animals that exist, imperfectly, as abstract types or mere links upon the evolutionary ladder. The hideous bird called the *cigana*, for example, which perches on the flexible boughs of the *oirana* willows bearing beneath wings capable of only short-distance flight a reptilian claw.

Thus is nature portentous but at the same time incomplete. It is a stupendous construct lacking in internal coherence. We must bear in mind that, if the calculations of Wallace and of Hartt are correct, the Amazon region may well be the world's newest land. It was born of the last geogenic upheaval, which raised the Andes and has barely finished its evolutionary process with the Quaternarian plains that are still forming and are preponderant within its unstable topography.

It contains everything and at the same time lacks everything, because it lacks that linking-together of phenomena developed within a rigorous process that produces the well-defined truths of art and of science—and which bespeaks the grand unconscious logic of things.

Hence this peculiar singularity: in all America, Amazonia is the region most studied and simultaneously least well known. From Humboldt to Emilio Goeldi—from the dawn of the past century to our own day—the best minds have scrutinized it intently. Read them. You will see that none ever ventured beyond the great vertebrating valley. And even there each took refuge in the shelter of a specialization that absorbed him. Wallace, Mawe, W. Edwards, d'Orbigny, Martius, Bates, Agassiz, to cite merely those who occur to me in first order, were in effect reduced to brilliant monograph writers.

Despite its abundance, the scientific literature on the Amazon reflects the physical geography of Amazonia: it is amazing, highly unusual and exceedingly disjointed. Any who dare study it carefully will, at the end of that attempt, get but a small way past the threshold to a marvelous world.

Professor Hartt had a phrase for the challenge that even robust spirits feel in the face of such an enormity. As he studied Amazonian geology, he found himself so thoroughly unmoored from the concise formulas of science and so carried away in dream that he suddenly felt obliged to lower the sails driving him toward fantasy: "I am not a poet. I speak the prose of my science. *Revenons!*"

Thus he rededicated himself to rigorous scientific deduction. But no more than two pages farther along he could hold out no longer and he set out again on his flight of fancy. The great river, despite its sovereign monotony, evokes the marvelous so powerfully that it catches up the unpresuming chronicler, the romantic adventurer, and the careful scholar alike. In the past, Orellana's Amazons, Guillaume de l'Isle's titanic *curriquerés*, and Walter Raleigh's Manoa del Dorado formed a fascinating mythological cycle of sorts. They are replicated today in the most imaginative of scientific hypotheses. The imagination can become hyperdeveloped when acting on a discordance in the land itself. Even the most ordered of minds can become unbalanced on inquiring into such grandeur. The results, in the area of objective research proper, are views such as Humboldt's and the conjectures through which the entire set of notions, from Wallace's dynamics of earthquakes to Agassiz's formidable biblical concept of antediluvian glaciers are either set forth or contested.

It would seem, then, that the expansive discourse characteristic of the analysis must have to do with the complexity of the problems: the flight of fancy can make easy use of induction, and truths can devolve into hyperbole. From time to time we idealize uncontrollably the tangible elements of a surprising reality, and the most unbridled dreamer may well find himself in perfect company with the most dedicated scholar.

One can accompany Katzer, for example, on his project to classify, analyze, and compare ancient petrified fossils by means of a long pilgrimage of mind through the most remote points of the oldest ages. To those who deliberate on the classificatory structure and search through the Greek roots of the nomenclature, the pronouncements of science can suddenly open out into a kind of idealism. Analyses end up in marvels; a microscope unveils a past multiple times millenarian. Those who focus on the stupendous outlines of a dead geography see spread out before their eyes the indeterminate spectacle of that extinct middle Devonian ocean that swamped the entire Mato Grosso and Bolivia, covering the bulk of South America, lapping in the west the ancient Goiás highlands, last remaining shoreline of the Brazilio-Eleopic continent that once linked to Africa and made what is now the Atlantic a land mass. Then one might follow the Morgan Commission naturalists, and geological history, despite its more reliable lineaments, will not be absent a touch of grandiosity as it unfolds along the length of the two banks of the huge Tertiary channel that for ages divided the high plains of Brazil from those of Guiana, until the slow rise of the Andes in the west walled off one of its ends and transformed it into a gulf, an estuary, a river.

Finally, if we continue to follow the current facts of Amazonian physiography, there are yet multiple other active factors that greatly disturb the cold serenity of scientific observation.

This brief survey will suffice to demonstrate that even in the simplest matters the Amazon presents a clear deviation from the usual evolution of topographic forms.

All land is a kind of block that is molded by external agents, among which the great rivers are primary remodelers of natural features. Compensating for the degradation of peaks with the raising of valleys, wearing down mountains and building up plains, they in general combine constructive and destructive processes in such a manner that landscapes, in their slow, constant transfiguration, manifest the effects of a prodigious sculpting process.

In this way the Huang Ho created a delta that became a province of China. And even more significantly the Mississippi astonishes the naturalist with its ongoing monumental redeposit of earth, which will soon reach depths that will connect with the Gulf Stream. Dissolved continents are contained in their silty waters. Countries are transformed. Lands are remade. And there is so logical a set of processes in their continuous great expenditure of natural energy that to observe them sometimes suggests observation of the lineaments of an aspect of human activity: from the pages of Herodotus to those of Maspero, one can contemplate the genesis of a civilization in parallel with the genesis of a delta. The parallel is so exact as seemingly to justify the exaggerated claims of such as Metchnikoff, who sees the great rivers as the principal causes of the development of nations.

With the Amazon the opposite is the case. What is foremost in it is the prohibitive, the destructive function. Its enormous volume destroys the land. Professor Hartt, impressed by its ever-muddy waters, calculated that "if a continuous train were running non-stop day and night on a railroad and it were loaded with mud and sand, that enormous quantity of matteryp would still be less than what is in fact transported by its waters."[1]

But that mass of dissolved earth is not redistributed. This greatest of rivers has no delta. Marajó Island, which supports a selective flora of plants adapted to their marismatic environment and the instability of the silt deposits, is a mirage land. If the vegetation were stripped away, all that would be left would be the scoured surface of the swampy, potholefilled *mondongos* stretching out to the water's edge. Alternately, craggy peaks of hardened sandstone randomly scattered across the surface of a bay. In the light of Walter Bates's rigorous deductions, which corroborate

Martius's prior conjecture, what exists under the cover of the forest is a ruin: the decomposed remnants of the land mass that once stretched from the coasts of Belém to the coasts of Macapá. It would have to be reconstituted in its ancient integrity to explain the identity that exists between the land fauna of northern Brazil and that of the Guianas, now separated by the great river.[2]

The Amazon could, however, reconstitute it in little time with the 3 million cubic meters of sediment that it bears within it every twenty-four hours. But instead it dissipates that cargo. At the end of its six-thousand-mile course, its turbid current becomes even muddier with earth breaking off from banks that continually collapse, making the shores that run from the Paru to the Araguari recede farther and farther apart. And all of it empties full into the Atlantic. What remains of the demolished islands—among them Caviana Island, which in times past had been the river's dam and then, during historical times, came to be divided in half—are slowly dissolving and disappearing amid the watery onslaught. Thus the principal mouth of this great artery is becoming increasingly less clogged, and its turn north is becoming more pronounced as it abandons the terrain to its east over which it once passed. In the process it is leaving in land recently liberated from the bogs of Marajó tangible evidence of a lateral move of the river bed itself, in which inexpert geologists have been deceived into seeing a raising or reconstruction of the land.

Because while the land is in fact reconstituted, that reconstitution takes place very far from our shores. For this river that more than any other defies our lyrical patriotism is in fact the least Brazilian of our watercourses. It is a strange adversary, given over day and night to the task of wearing away its own land. Herbert Smith, deceived by the powerful mass of muddy water that the traveler observes at high sea even before glimpsing Brazil itself, imagined that it had a truly prodigious task: that of building a new continent. He explained as follows: the deposit of that amount of sediment on the tranquil floor of the Atlantic Ocean would create new lands in the sea, and at the end of a millennarian process the open gulf that arcs from Cape Orange to the point of the Gurupi would be filled. Thereby the lands of Pará would be considerably expanded to the northeast.[3]

"The king is building his monument," the enraptured naturalist exclaimed, casting in harsh, Britannic syllables a flight of fancy that would surprise the most irrepressible of Latin souls. He did not bear in mind, however, that this most original of hydrographic systems does not stop with the land but passes Cabo do Norte and continues on without banks far into the sea in search of the equatorial current, which it joins, turning over to it that huge load of matter capable of generating lands. That matter, distributed by that immense ocean current which ends up in the Gulf Stream, emerges in concentrated doses in far-flung places from the coastlines of the Guianas, where lagoons are created, beginning in Amapá, that progressively dry into steppes advancing inland from the sea to the coastal regions of Georgia and the Carolinas in North America—regions that continue to grow in a way that cannot be explained as the effect of the short watercourses that run down the eastern slopes of the Alleghenies.

In such places the Brazilian, albeit a foreigner, would be treading Brazilian land. Which leads to an astounding perplexity: to the fiction of extraterritorial law—country without land—is counterposed another basic physical concept—land without country. Such is the marvelous effect of this other kind of telluric migration. Land abandons man. It goes in search of other climes. And the Amazon, in constructing its actual delta in such remote areas as another hemisphere, bespeaks the unrecognized voyage of earth in motion, changing with the passage of time, never stopping even for a second, and shrinking, in an uninterrupted process of deterioration, the great land surfaces over which it travels.

The river's process cannot have enduring or fixed formations attributed to it. At places along the circuitous channel the water pools, and the earth within it settles out, along with the seeds it contains. Then the river's productive capacity comes surprisingly to the fore. The recently formed shoal eventually breaks the surface and begins to deploy itself in an indiscernible profile. Then it defines itself forcefully; it rises higher and widens, gently redirecting the water. And on the island thus created, visibly growing and building on itself, crowded with *cabucho* vines that twist and stretch out over the surface like the tentacles of some prodigious organism, a struggle among plant species plays out that is so vital and so dramatic that the confusion of twisting stalks, stems, and boughs comprises all the movements in an enormous, silent conflict. They stretch out, convulsively intermingling, intertwining. From the patches of dumb cane that hold together the amorphous clay with their networking rhizomes, to the mangroves that supplant the dumb cane, pushing it off to the edges with violent and tumultuous activity, to the vertical palms that in turn crowd out the mangroves, relegating them to the swampy margins and taking control of the solider high ground.

Cururu Island, with an area of two square kilometers, recently came into being in this very manner. So too are built all the islands that one can see above the Breves channels.

But they are thus formed only to be destroyed or ceaselessly relocated. Worn away by the very currents that produced them, the islands are decomposed upstream and reconstituted farther down, slowly navigating downstream like monstrous, mastless pontoons with long, shrunken prows and high sterns, traveling night and day at an imperceptible rate of speed. Eventually they come apart and end. The island of Urucuritiba lasted in that manner for ten years, from 1840 to 1850, thanks to its enormous surface area. It came to its end in a season of high water.

The same process takes place on the shores. The Amazon's banks do not channel its powerful flow. They are instead banks that avoid the river. They normally remain at the edge of its vast plain dotted with "solid ground lakes," which compensatorily mitigate the violence of the flood during high water. Here there can develop a kind of large-scale earthworks construction. The river, which runs in multiple courses and eddies during high water, overflows its banks and discharges itself onto the welcoming plains. It uproots entire forests, piling tree trunks and brush in the numerous depressions in the flatland. The calm water deposits the debris in a widely generalized settling-out process across the watery flood plain, or *várzea*. When the water recedes, one sees that the land has visibly increased. It gains height from one high-water season to the next, the tall "walls" rising, the marshlands and sloughs drying up, to define the rising lands called *firmes*, which are then invaded by the triumphant flora . . . until, at a new high water, this entire lateral delta is torn down again in a single assault.

On the night of July 29, 1866, the "fallen land" along the left bank of the Amazon constituted a continuous line fifty leagues in length.

It is an ancient, invariable process manifest over the short course of our history. The high embankment of the ancient shores of the Paru, where the legendary Amazons appeared to Orellana's mercenaries, is today reduced to a degraded shoal visible only at extreme low water.

The river's extreme variability is also profiled in its endless, maddeningly confused twists and turns. They resemble the uncertain path that might be taken by a lost wanderer guessing at directions, turning every which way, suddenly throwing himself along a course arbitrarily chosen. Thus has the river cast itself through the stifling Óbidos narrows in total abandonment of its ancient bed, which can be glimpsed today in the immense marismatic plain of Vila Franca, gangliated with ponds. In other places it flows into its own great tributaries through the unpredictable *furos*, thereby, illogically becoming a tributary of its own tributaries. Ever disorganized, turbulent, vacillating, tearing down, building up, rebuilding and leveling, devastating in an hour what it spent decades building— with the eagerness, the agony, and the exasperation of a monstrous artist ever unsatisfied, taking up again, redoing, perpetually beginning anew a painting without end.

Such is the river, then, and such its history: tumultuous, disorganized, incomplete.

The wild Amazonian region has always had the gift of impressing far-off civilization. From the earliest years of the colony the most imposing of expeditions and most solemn of pastoral visits have sought its unknown lands preferentially. To it have come the most venerable bishops, elegant captains, and lucid scientists. From the tilling of a soil to cultivate exotic crops to developing the aborigine to raise him to the highest destiny, the distant metropole outdid itself in efforts to open up this land that above all others would compensate it for the lost, prodigious India.

Efforts all in vain. The demarcation parties, the apostolic missions, the government voyages with their hundreds of canoes and their astronomers supplied with complex instruments, and their prelates, and their warriors intermittently penetrated these solitary recesses and set up on the flatlands atop the "walls" the sumptuous tents of civilization at travel. They promulgated rules for cultivation, for civilizing of the people, and for beautification of the land.

Then they went on to other parts, or back home . . . and in their *malocas* the locals, transfigured for a moment, abruptly fell away, returning to their original brutishness.

At the end of the eighteenth century, Alexandre Rodrigues Ferreira made a "philosophical voyage" along the main course of the great river and found himself traveling amid ruins. In the village of Barcelos, capital of that remote district, he encountered the tangible image of a typically Amazonian progress in the proud Palace of the Demarcations: grand, imposing, monumental, and covered with cogongrass! It was symbolic.

Everything is vacillating, ephemeral, paradoxical in this strange land where the cities are as nomadic as the people, ever relocating as the ground beneath them continually disappears, undermined by the currents or collapsing in "fallen lands."

Century after century passes with intolerable sameness: stubborn attempts later aborted. The most lucid observers' impressions remain the same, ever discouraging in the face of the spectacle of a deplorable present in comparison with the illusion of a glorious past.

In 1852, when the province of Amazonas was created, Tenreiro Aranha assumed leadership of it. In a retrospective assessment referring to the extinct industry of "high-quality manufacture," he tells us of the extraordinary progress that was lost:

> cotton, indigo, manioc, and coffee were cultivated in such a way that local consumption was supported and there was a remainder for export. Hence the indigo manufactories, the establishments making palm rope, the mills producing yarn, cloth, and net out of cotton, straw, and feathers; the tiles and masonry; civil and naval construction, with able workers building temples, palaces, or imposing ships.

If we go back another century in search of that wonderful time, however, we discover with great disappointment, in a report produced by another illustrious governor, Captain-General Furtado de Mendonça, that the "captaincy was reduced to the utmost ruin." Thus evaluations stand at odds with each other while registering the same disappointment. Or they can be seen as resoundingly agreeing on the subject of the decadence of the area's bizarre inhabitants. In 1762, the bishop of Grão-Pará, the remarkable Brother João de São José—Voltairean Benedictine whose writing style possessed the pyrotechnics of a Padre Vieira—inventoried the people and things "so as to establish that the root cause of the vices of this land is sloth." He described summarily the inhabitants with these discouraging words: "lasciviousness, drunkenness, and thievery." If one wished to know if the state of affairs had improved a hundred years later, one might merely leaf through the austere pages of Wallace and note that they seem merely to translate, all but literally, the astute Benedictine's words: what the astonished scholar sees pass before his eyes is an undisciplined society based on "drinking, gambling, and lying" amid a lack of awareness about life.

Thus sinful indifference to the higher attributes, systematic rejection of scruples, and a heart all too given to error are centuries old here and arise from a painful historical apprenticeship that runs from the *casa do paricá* to the huts of the rubber tappers. Read through our old chroniclers, especially the imaginative Father João Daniel, and you will see the impediments to physical and moral motivation that have long served to weaken the character of the people living here. And read Tenreiro Aranha, José Veríssimo, and scores of others. Those books contain fragmentary scenes of some of history's greatest dramas of dissolution.

Then there is the intractable factor of physical destiny. Sovereign and brutal nature in full application of its energies is an adversary to the human being. In that perpetual steam bath to which Bates refers, one can easily understand the tendency toward a vegetative life of ease and risk avoidance. It is harder to imagine here that intricate resonance of a spirit involved in the dynamic of ideas or that superior tension of will that takes place in acts that derive from impulses other than the merely egotistical. I do not exaggerate. A talented Italian physician, Dr. Luigi Buscalione, recently spent some time in the Amazon and characterized the effects of climate on the outsider as, first, hyperexcitement of the psychic and sensual functions and, second, an accompanying slow weakening of all the faculties, starting with the most noble.[4]

But in this appeal to the classic concept of climatic influence he omitted, as have many others, the weight—likely of secondary importance but hardly negligible—of the very transitoriness of the physical foundations on which the society stands.

The changeability of the river infects the human being. In the Amazon, what generally takes place is the following: the observer who wanders the basin in search of its varied perspectives, at the end of hundreds of miles, derives the impression that they have circled about in a closed loop filled with the same beaches and walls and islands, the same forests and stagnant sloughs called *igapós* stretching out to empty horizons farther than the eye can see. By contrast, the observer who stays at the margins is intermittently astonished by unexpected transformations. Scenes that are repetitive in the realm of space change over time. To the eyes of the person in motion nature is stable; to the eyes the sedentary person whose project it may be to subject that nature to the stability of human cultivation, it seems frighteningly changeable and fragile, and the appearance of that mutability occasionally overwhelms him. It almost always ends up terrifying him and driving him away.

Adaptation is exercised through nomadism. Hence, in great part, the paralysis, simultaneously disordered and sterile, of the people who for three centuries have wandered here.

To its collective psychology today, the Amazon should refer back, in its entirety, to the old dolorous aphorism created by Barleaus in colonial times to describe its excesses: "Away from the equator I never sinned."

Amazonians perceive this in their being. At the entrance to Manaus lies beautiful Marapatá Island. The island, however, has an alarming function. It is the most original of quarantine stations—a quarantine station for the soul! They say that the new arrival leaves their conscience there . . . Let the implications of that product of popular fancy be well measured. That island across from the mouth of the Purus has lost its old geographical name and is simply called Conscience Island. The same occurs with a similar island at the mouth of the Juruá. On entering through the two portals that lead to the diabolical paradise of the rubber tracts, man abdicates the highest of the qualities with which he is born and laughingly condemns himself with that formidable irony. In fact, within the exuberant climes of the rubber-producing trees there awaits him the most heinous organization of labor ever conjured up by human egotism unbound.

The rubber tapper—I do not mean the wealthy owner but rather the actual practitioner subject to the realm of the "paths" along which he harvests—engages in a portentous anomaly: he is the man who toils in order to enslave himself.

Some cold, reliable numbers reveal the enormity of the situation.

Behold the following account of the selling of a man.

On the very day he sets out from Ceará the rubber tapper goes into debt: he owes the cost of his passage in steerage to Pará (35,000 reis) and the advance he has received for the trip (150,000). Then comes the cost of travel, in whatever craft is available, from Belém to the distant outpost for which he is bound: on average, another 150,000. Add roughly 800,000 for standard utensils: one large funnel jar, one basin, a thousand small bowls, an iron ax, a saber, a Winchester carbine and two hundred bullets, two plates, two spoons, two cups, two pots, a coffee pot, two spools of linen thread, and a needle case. Just those things and nothing more. The man is now arrived at the owner's headquarters, or *barracão*, soon to leave for the individual hut in the forest that will be assigned him. He is a greenhorn—someone who has not yet learned how to cut trees. And he already owes 1,135,000 reis. He will go out to his solitary post, to be followed by a transport that will bring the baggage and supplies, his name scrupulously inscribed on them, that will have to last him three months: three panniers of mandioc flour, one sack of beans, another (small) of salt, twenty kilos of rice, thirty of jerky, twenty-one of coffee, thirty of sugar, six tins of lard, eight pounds of tobacco, and twenty grams of quinine. All this costs him approximately 750,000 reis. He has not yet put a hatchet mark on a single tree, he is still the unskilled greenhorn mocked by the experienced *manso*, and he has already invested 2,090,000 reis.

Let us now presume a set of favorable conditions, which almost never actually occur: (1) our rubber tapper is single; (2) he gets to his post in May, at the beginning of the tapping season; (3) he does not fall ill, for then he would have to be brought back to the *barracão* for treatment, at the cost of 10,000 reis a day; (4) he buys nothing beyond the afore-mentioned supplies—and he is serious, tenacious, incorruptible: stoically embarked on fortune's road with a clear eye to a long, painful penitence. Let us go even further: let us allow that, despite his lack of experience, he manages to extract 350 kilos of high-quality latex and 100 kilos of the coarse *sernambi* over the year—which is difficult, at least in the Purus area.

When the harvest is over, this tenacious, stoical man, this rare individual, is still a debtor. According to the terms of the standard contract, it is the owner who sets the price of the product and does the accounts. The 350 kilos, purchased on the spot at 5,000 a kilo, bring 1,750,000 reis. The 100 kilos of *sernambi*, at 2,500 a kilo, 250,000. Total: 2,000,000 reis.

Our tapper is still a debtor and is unlikely ever to get free of that status. The next season he will be a *manso*. He will have learned the ins and outs of the job and can extract 600 to 700 kilos. But he will have been inactive throughout the high-water season from November to May—seven months in which simple subsistence costs more than twice what he has in supplies: in round figures, 1,500,000 reis. In the second year let us assume that he does not need to replace any equipment or cloth-ing and does not become ill. Even in this rarest of cases, unusual is the harvester who is able to earn his way out.

Now look at the real situation. That kind of fighter is exceptional. The man usually brings to these lands the lack of foresight typical of our race. He often brings his family along, which compounds his burden; he almost always falls ill because of the general incontinence.

In addition to all this is the disastrously one-sided contract the owner imposes. The regulations of the rubber tracts are painfully indicative in this regard. To read them is to witness the rebirth of a crude, humiliating feudalism. The owner sets forth, obstinately, with stupendous grammatical inflexibility, some astonishing decrees. For example, the following heinous crimes bring with them the onerous fine of 100,000 reis:

a. Making a cut in the tree shallower than the width of the hatchet blade
b. Taking the plug out of the wood when cutting it
c. Tapping with hatchets that have a handle more than four palms long

In addition, the worker can make purchases only at the headquarters store, being "prohibited from making purchases elsewhere under penalty of a 50-percent fine upon the total amount of the purchase." Let us be done once and for all with such brutal pronouncements! Compared to this, Caliban's terrible stammer is almost musical.

At the end of some years this contract laborer, or *freguês*, will be irretrievably lost. His debt will have risen to alarming levels: 3, 4, 5, sometimes 10 million reis, which he will never be able to repay. He then finds himself in the dead end of unprotected indentured servitude. The relevant regulation is pitiless: "no *freguês* or negotiator will be allowed to leave without paying in full all of his commercial transactions." Flee? Don't even think it. The immense distance to be traversed is forbidding. Find another *barracão?* The owners have an agreement among themselves not to take another's employee until that employee's debts have been satisfied in full. In the Acre not long ago there was a widely attended meeting held to systematize that alliance, in which it was decided that any owner who might show recalcitrance on this score would himself be subject to heavy fines.

Now tell me, what does the intrepid *sertanejo* attracted to these climes in search of riches have left at the end of a five-year period?

He is not even allowed to put down roots in the land. An article in the same infamous regulations makes him an eternal guest in his own house. Let me cite it in its grotesque, savage and imbecilic formulation: All improvements performed on said property by one whose contract has been terminated will be forfeit upon his departure.

Hence the painful appearance that the small huts present. The traveler who looks for them can barely make out the faint path leading through the wild banana trees to the dwelling half choked by the bush. The man who dwells there invests no effort to improve a place from which he can be expelled at any time with no right of appeal.

Although painful examples could be adduced to accompany this overview, going through them would be useless. What comes definitively to the fore is the urgent need for measures to rescue this hidden, abandoned culture: a work law that ennobles human effort; an austere justice that curbs excesses; and some form of homestead provision that definitively links man and land.

NOTES

1. Charles Frederick Hartt, "A geologia do pará," *Diário do Grão Pará*, 1870.
2. Walter Bates, *The Naturalist on the River Amazon* (London, 1892), 55–56.
3. Herbert Smith, *The Amazons and the Coast* (New York, 1879), 2–3.
4. Luigi Buscalione, *Una escursione botanica nell'amazzonia* (Roma, 1901). Republication of "Escursione botanica in Brasile," *Bollettino della Società Geografica Italiana* (Rome) 4, no. 2 (1901): 1, 3, 4–5.

Rivers in Abandon

The American geographer William Morris Davis has revealed the "life cycle" of rivers. His was a revolutionary idea; there was not a scientist wedded to the passé descriptive geography still dominant among us who was not scandalized by the Yankee's bold concept. That antagonism, however, was short-lived and feeble. In a single stroke, one simple monograph, *The Rivers and Valleys of Pennsylvania* (1889), reordered the thrust of what had preceded it and staked out a new direction in geographical analysis. It did so by linking river form with structure of terrain, thereby complementing interpretation of the impassive *facies* with geological analysis, and by explaining the causes of the most transitory features and discovering in the visible lines of the earth's changing physiognomy the eloquent expression of the natural energies that had molded it and continue ceaselessly to transform it. In the end it surprised no one that Davis, carrying his new doctrine out to its ultimate implications, arrived at a kind of monstrous physiology and dramatically described the complex vicissitudes of the millennarian existence of our teeming watercourses, revealing them to be possessed of an ebullient infancy, a rebellious adolescence, a self-controlled maturity, and a melancholy old age or decrepitude, as though they were stupendous organisms subject to the laws of competition and selection leading to triumph or annihilation more or less in accordance with how well they adapt to external conditions.

It is not my intent here merely to repeat the ingenious biographer of the rivers of Pennsylvania by explaining his admirable theory, which represents a case of an impressive charge, a daring "rush" of imagination and fantasy, within the quiet sanctuaries of science. One needs only note that it has been generally accepted and rests on solid inductive data.

Despite the variations of theater in which they operate, all watercourses pass through inevitable stages in regular rhythms. At first indecisive, errant, fragile, they run according to chance among topographical features, as though seeking a cradle in each and every low area of the land, gathering in numerous incoherently distributed lakes, where they come to rest. Then, when their first regular carved-out drainage troughs become defined channels into which the water from the rains flows and gathers, currents form, carving out incipient beds and initiating, with the tumultuous energy of the cataracts, a centuries-long stage of clash with the solidity of the earth. Finally, when the structural obstacles are overcome, a course is established and a riverbed defined, the river is fully constituted, with its stable tributaries, a continuous slope descending in regular curves, a thalweg adjusted to the contexture of the soil and to the morphological differentiation that reflects its various segments—from the headwaters where the wild flows of its former torrential regime remain, to the midcourse, which characterizes its current stage of development, to the lower stretch, which prefigures its decrepitude and where it spreads out to build, with the settling out of the silt that it bears imperceptibly, the very alluvial plain through which it runs.

This is the phase of maturity. The river is in the plenitude of its life, after the complex molding of all its features is complete. It reaches that stage at the end of a persistent struggle that sometimes comprises the entire geological history of the region through which it flows.

There has not been a single point in all the trajectory of hundreds if not thousands of kilometers that it did not attack, no single grain of sand that it did not move, balancing its upstream excavations with its downstream deposits, constructing itself in consonance with the universal tendency toward stable states. It has finally acquired its balanced longitudinal profile, which, still steep in the high areas where the flow is fastest and the volume lowest, continuously diminishes along the course of its fall until it reaches the near-horizontal base level of its mouth. At that point the elements are reversed, and the system's dynamic equilibrium is reached by the inverse relationship between liquid mass and speed of flow.

Whatever the details, once it reaches this stage the elements of its thalweg, projected onto the vertical plane, approximate the shape of one arm of a gigantic parabola with its curve opening upward.

That is the geometrical expression of a complex mechanical fact. And while the tendency toward that figure may often be distorted or contravened in areas of variable resistance, where the rocks that the river has revealed protrude and create the antagonism of the cataracts, in the areas of homogeneous terrain the parabolic curve is clearly described as the definitive form of the longitudinal section of all rivers at the end of their tribulated evolution.

One of the best examples is provided by the Purus. If we graph its profile over its entire 3,210-kilometer course, from the point where it empties into the Solimões back to its most remote sources in the Pucani branch in the low, nameless mountains that divide the largest hydrographic basins on earth, we come up with approximately that parabolic arm.

At very least, no other form of curve would describe it better.

The following table, in which the various stretches of the Purus are listed one after the other in the sequence of its consistent fall along its course, demonstrates as much:

Sections	Itinerary Distances	Difference in Level	General Slope	Slope per Km
From headwaters to the Curiuja	117 km	189 m	1/619	1.6 m
From the Curiuja to Curanja	278 km	60 m	1/4500	0.22 m
From Curanja to the mouth of the Chandless	304 km	49 m	1/6500	0.16 m
From the Chandless to the mouth of the Yaco	300 km	39 m	1/7700	0.13 m
From the Yaco to the Acre	237 km	27 m	1/8700	0.115 m
From the Acre to the Pani	233 km	20 m	1/11000	0.085 m
From the Pani to the Mucuím	740 km	58 m	1/12900	0.077 m
From the Mucuím to the Solimões	990 km	15 m	1/66700	0.015 m

There is only one questionable datum in the chart: the difference in level between the beginning and the end of the last stretch. It has been supplied deductively by the use of a minimal figure of eighteen meters above sea level for the mouth of the Purus, although the actual height is surely greater than that—and therefore even more supportive of the conclusion. The remainder of the data are owing to the work of William Chandless and to my own recent observations.

Even the most cursory glance at the chart, without resort to reductionism, reveals that, traversing a homogeneous and more or less impermeable terrain with a slope that, while relatively gentle, is typical on the vast plain, where rainfall is very evenly distributed, the great river parallels Davis's theoretical conditions very closely. And as it finishes its geological evolution it is admirably described by the majestic figure of the parabola, introduced above.

If we study its general regimen, then, we shall be doing so with the solid grounding of someone dealing with the equation of a curve.

Thus, when we consider the first stretch, its 1.6 meters per kilometer fall, so different from the 0.22 of the following stretch, it immediately tells us, without our needing to engage in site study, that the true Upper Purus, officially designated as beginning at Boca do Acre and put by some geographers even further downstream, in fact begins much further up: at 3019 kilometers from the river mouth. It begins at the confluence of the Cujar and the Curiúja, the two tributaries of which it partakes equally, there losing its name and being divided up over and over again at one of the most remote points in its vast catch basin.

Nevertheless, the real fall of 1/619 scarcely approaches the recognized ratio of 1/500 established as the lower limit of torrents.

It can, then, be immediately concluded that the river, even in its highest stretch, where the creation of regularized river beds always takes the longest and is the most difficult, is at a very advanced stage of development. It is the exception among great river arteries—among the largest on earth, navigable even during extreme high water, when the flood covers the numerous levels of its rapids. Even then, assuming that the water rises three meters in a ten-meter channel, with that fall of .0016 meters per meter simple use of D'Aubuisson's formula shows us that the currents will run with a maximum speed of only 23.2 meters, a speed against which a strong launch can easily make headway.

These first-calculation conclusions about a picture so straightforward that a supporting diagram is rendered unnecessary are obvious to the eyes of even the most unobservant of explorers who might venture there after a five-hundred-league trek through the Amazonian plain.

In fact, what especially impresses a person in that situation is the spectacle of the land, deeply carved out by the incommensurable, ongoing action of the river's formative elements. After walking the Pucani's serpentine canyon to the foot of the last slopes, he comes to the escarpment of a series of insignificant, broken-down hills. Their height of barely sixty meters can be climbed in three short minutes. The traveler cannot believe he finds himself at one of the most extraordinary hydrographic borders on the globe: here he can take one step and go from the Amazon Valley to the Ucayali Valley.

The height at which he finds himself is at best unimpressive. Indeed, it is insufficient for him to see horizons or make out distances. There is no comprehending it with even the best topographical map. He doubtless will never understand how so indecisive a *divortium acquarum* can exist in relation to two such massive river arteries, if, in seeking out those distant reaches, penetrating, braving the boulders accumulated along the resculpted channels of the Cujar, the Cavaljani, and the Pucani, he does not dedicate himself to attentive contemplation of the powerful dynamic of the waters and the effect they have in transforming a site previously higher and more dominant. He should not concern himself with lack of paleontological knowledge or the absence of indicative fossils. He obviously is located at the ruins of an almost extinct high point, one whose syncline he could reconstruct by extending the lines of the strata revealed in the troughs in which those first tributaries run. In relative tranquility, almost stagnated between the intervals of their rapids (vestiges of ancient waterfalls now destroyed), they all reveal the last phase of struggle in which the Purus, to lengthen its section of stability, had to wear away mountains. The erosive activity and volume of matter washed away from all those slopes had to have been all but incalculable for the drainage courses to be worn all the way down to the rocky substratum and to be reduced, as we have seen, to a slope appropriate to navigable watercourses.

In spite of this, the transition to the subsequent stretch is sudden and involves a change in fall from 1.6 meters per kilometer to 0.22.

But that is the only such leap. Thereafter, as the preceding table shows, down to the last stretch that ends at river's mouth, where to go down a meter one has to traverse 66.7 meters, the decline in the rate of fall proceeds with perfect regularity. The Purus is thus to be included among those completely regularized watercourses whose advancing life cycle is coming to an end.

The bed is not being dug out deeper. The appearance of sandstone outcroppings at low water at various places between Huitanaá and the mouth of the Acre, and from there with lesser frequency on up to just a little beyond the Yaco, reinforces that analysis even though it seems to do the opposite. Remaining stretches of old rapids, now largely dismantled, stand as witnesses to the early erosion. In general, they no longer have that effect. The little town of Cachoeira ("Cataract"), sited as it is along a tranquil stretch of the river, would appear to have the most inappropriate of names. But it is one indicative of an accident lost in the remote geological past. Only a few blocks jumbled into tiny reefs and small "bars" remain of it. Here the same picture of the land as in other stretches, land stretching out flat in all directions or softly undulating to reveal modeling completed, combines with the other features to suggest the last phase in the valley's evolutionary process.

Only one element is lacking: regularity in the level of the opposing banks along the succession of bends in the river. A cross-section of the Purus usually shows a low beach struggling to slope up to the distant heights of a low plain opposite a steep bank such as one finds on the shore opposite the mouth of the Chandless or a precipitous wall, as in the remarkable situation of the Cataí.

The fact is that the constancy of the river's profile of equilibrium stands in opposition to the variability of its course to an extent that gives cause to those who include the Purus among those rivers "whose beds and banks are not describable with a defined and established structure."

In fact, the Purus, one of the most winding watercourses on earth, is also one of the most variable as regards its bed. In contemporary geographical terms it "wanders." The continuous reduction in the velocity of its flow, until it reaches near stagnation in the area of its mouth, along with the instability of the alluvial lands through which it flows—created by it with the materials it bears downstream from its sources—determine this character of variability. Its waters, flowing in weak eddies, lack the motion necessary to create a straight course. The least impediment shunts them aside. The slight blockage created by such as the trunk of a silk-cotton tree fallen from one of the banks redirects the watery mass over against the opposite bank, where it quickly produces a deep erosion with dramatic effects, less by the actual force of the flow than as the result of the instability of the terrain.

The aimless twisting and turning thereby formed deploys itself in ever greater loops that increase the force of the centrifugal dimension of the current, which in turn carves out a growing concavity. The end result is that within a few years the entire river moves laterally from its prior course. But given that the former course had been traced out in concert with the determining elements in a profile of inviolable equilibrium, that move can never be a bifurcation or a definitive change. After cutting out a huge, eroded circle, the river seeks to return to its old channel, like someone who has merely maneuvered around an obstacle in their path.

The circle through which the river has detoured now tends to close. As a result, all the affected terrain is transformed into a veritable peninsula linked to the main land by an isthmus that is often so narrow that the sojourner could cross it in minutes. He would need an entire day in a boat, however, to navigate its almost "islanded" shoreline. As the next step, it is completely cut off, becoming a true island: during a high water season the Purus breaches the fragile wall of the isthmus and all at once reclaims its prior course, leaving behind on one side, as a remembrance of the detour through which it had once flowed, a curve-shaped lake—often a very large one. And it continues on, repeating such capricious meanderings as it goes, ones that always end up creating similar *sacados*. And so it proceeds, perpetually oscillating through the terrain lateral to its invariable axis, in a rhythm perfectly reflective of the interplay of mechanical laws susceptible of synthesis into a formula that would be the translation into analytical terms of a curious pendular movement across a level plane.

This process represents a natural solution to one of the most serious problems in river hydraulics. The lakes thus created are veritable dikes with a dual function: on the one hand they impede devastating floods by taking in excess high water; on the other hand, they regulate the rivers' regimen during the long periods of low water, for then they open by their own action, "bursting," in the local jargon, and return to a river impoverished by the scarcity of flow part of the liquid mass that they had been holding in reserve.

The value of these colossal works of nature is incalculable.

An illustrative comparison demonstrates. French hydraulicists who in 1856 reported a 10.9 meter rise in the waters of the Garonne as the cause of one of the most disastrous floods ever to occur in Europe, and who saw that rise as an unbelievable figure, would certainly not even comprehend the very working of the vast Amazonian terrain along the Purus (which, at high water, amounts to almost 50 Garonnes) if they knew that it rises fifteen meters at its mouth, which in addition is a mile wide, and that from there upstream at the confluence of the Acre the rise increases to a frightening twenty-three meters above the low water mark.

And that these periods of high water are nonetheless harmless.

With the first rains the fluid mass rises, rapidly climbing up the sides of the banks, and in a few days it beats against the posts that support the *barracões* built on the highest *firmes* in the area . . . and all that flow in motion does not flood, does not become a tumult, does not fly into dizzying cascades, does not swamp boats in swirling vortexes, and does not devastate the land. It spreads out; it expends itself silently; it discharges itself harmlessly in those thousands of safety valves. And, stretching out flat across the forest floor or spreading expansively across immense surfaces pockmarked with the last leafy spikes of foliage sticking up from the marshland now inundated, it instead renews that very land itself, adding year after year to its height with the perfect deposit of the silt it bears.

Thus, across that entire plain, this remarkable Amazonian tributary, twisting and turning its way in the innumerable serpentines that make its itinerary length twice its geographical length, is one of the world's most interesting "working rivers." It builds the submersible dikes that relieve it in high water—and intermittently rechannel it on both banks. Be they near the river or distant, they dot the *várzea*, becoming larger and more numerous as the river descends and the slopes decline, until the large basin located at Canutama is reached. There the great tranquil waters flow majestically in balance, dividing in half the flat immensity of a sprawling Mediterranean.

But this formation of lakes, or natural reservoirs, the beneficial role of which we have glimpsed, gives rise to liabilities so great that at some points they make almost impenetrable this watery artery that, seen as regards its positive features, compares favorably with those rivers most accessible to regular navigation.

In its persistent erosion of its banks in order to twist and turn as it does in its innumerable meanders, the Purus clogs itself with the roots and trunks of the trees that grow alongside it.

Sometimes a kilometers-long single stretch of "wall" breaks away all at once and abruptly drops an entire forest into the river.

It is an extremely regular occurrence. Everyone who lives in the area is familiar with it. It is not uncommon for the traveler to awake at night shaken by the earthquake-like tremors. He is stunned in fright as he immediately thereafter hears the indescribable crash of myriads of fronds, branches, and trunks, cracking, breaking, and falling all at the same time in a prolonged dull thud that calls to mind the death-dealing assault of a cataclysm and a tearing-away of the earth.

These are the "fallen lands," from which two kinds of obstacle always result. On the one hand, the heap of tangled tree trunks and branches either intertwined at the water's surface or breaking through that surface from below at dangerous points. On the other hand, the clay or clay-sand mass that the sluggish current does not dissolve, thereby allowing it to accumulate in the tiny islets called *torrões*, or, even more dangerously, in the low, compact banks called *salões*, which render the river unsuitable for passage even by vessels of very shallow draft.

There is no need to belabor this fact.

Its importance is obvious. And we must bear in mind that such impediments are continuously accumulating, at a faster and ever increasing rate, along the entire 480-kilometer extension from the mouth of the Yaco to the mouth of the Curiújá. One is therefore forced to conclude that the Purus, gifted with the basic requisite features and an unusual stability of regime, and having attained one of the most regular profiles in all hydrography thereby standing as a model among those rivers best suited to navigation, is now gradually losing a great part of those superior attributes in the face of progressive large-scale blockage, which will eventually render it completely impassable.

That statement is made on the basis of painstaking experience, which in fact culminated in shipwreck. Especially above the mouth of the Chandless, those barriers totally out of character with the special "tectonics" of the river are so frequent that over long stretches that have a depth of five to six feet at low water and over which the most powerful launches could pass fully loaded down, a light canoe can now scarcely slide. I shall desist from exhaustive exemplification of these passing considerations. But let me first merely note that from the aforementioned tributary to the Cujar-Curiújá split, at various places the Purus seems to run over the top of an ancient thicket. It seems to flow among the barkless, twisted branches of a dead forest. And if we observe that, in addition to the hazards they themselves present, these underwater palisades, impeding the river's flow as it filters through the interwoven branches, enable the formation of all kinds of shoals, we can understand the fullest prejudicial implications of this ongoing process of obstruction.

For the men who labor there—the Peruvian *caucho* harvester wielding his large paddles in his fast canoes, our own *seringueiro*, with the poles with which to push along his dugout, or the river trader from any country who does business there in slow lighters pulled along by tow—none of them invests any effort whatsoever to improve their one and only, magnificent roadway. They traverse over and over again the same dangerous topography. A thousand times they find their canoe in a tree trunk fallen ten years earlier along a river channel. A thousand times they wind their way with great difficulty into snarled thickets where twisted undergrowth bars their passage at every turn. They come ashore and laboriously drag canoes over the same *salões* of hardened clay. Countless times they risk shipwreck amid the water's noise as the result of running their dugouts against the hardened protrusions of the tree trunks that menace, invisibly, a palm's depth under the water's surface. But they expend against any of those sticks not the least effort whatsoever—not even the first knife cut or ax blow—toward the goal of uncluttering their passage.

The launches, even steamboats, that have begun to appear here more frequently, in transporting the harvest from the 120 prosperous rubber tracts that have established themselves upstream from the confluence of the Yaco, invariably make their trips during the favorable times of high water, when the impediments are submerged a number of meters below the surface.

They trek rapidly upstream. At various stopping points they hastily unload the merchandise consigned to them. They take on their cargo of latex. And then they return in flight back downstream. Despite this practice, some of them will not have ensured themselves against sudden drops in water level and they will find themselves trapped. And there they stay long months, awaiting the next high water, or the unlikely event of a propitious flash flood, wintering over, paradoxically, under blazing sun—and in the most curious situations. Sometimes right in the river, held fast by the hundreds of the branches of dead trees. Sometimes halfway up an embankment, where they had been surprised by the receding water, stranded at clumsy angles, their prows dug into the dirt, aimed downhill in permanent danger of falling. Sometimes atop a wall like authentic ghost ships seemingly prepared to sail off into the majestic forest at a moment's notice.

The contrast between river traffic carried out this way and the magnificent technical conditions that the Purus offers could not be more glaring. Just like all the southern tributaries of the Amazon except the Madeira, as regards care the Purus has been entirely abandoned.

Nevertheless, the very terms of the exposition of these difficulties, in clear contradistinction to the favorable structural conditions, makes it clear that the removal of the obstacles, while painstaking, does not require any exceptional engineering feats or any extraordinary expense.

What there is for man to do is straightforward and simple.

The river itself has taken care of the serious problems of river hydraulics, through the harmonious interplay of the natural forces that created it.

And they constitute an incalculable accomplishment. The Purus is one of the greatest gifts among the great number that scandalously profligate nature has pressed upon us.

Let us take a quick look.

River hydraulics came into being between the beds of the Garonne and the Loire, so great and so many are the monuments that French engineering has erected in that space. Never before has man labored with such persistence and such brilliance against the brute force of the elements. The Roman transformation of the area of Algeria and Dutch construction of Holland are apt parallels to the efforts of the selfless professionals who, over an entire century, undaunted by successive setbacks, devoted themselves to the overwhelming task of taming torrents, containing floods, and controlling avalanches—with the dual goal of facilitating navigation and protecting shoreline terrain. All that magnificent undertaking, in which the names of Deschamps, Dieulafoy, and Belgrand have been immortalized, have proven largely fruitless, however. Fruitless or even counterproductive. The masterpieces of engineering science actually ended up damaging the Loire.

The submersible or insubmersible dikes designed to protect towns, the overflow canals that were linked to them, the artificial banks that lined scores of kilometers of the smallest streambeds, the rock placements to counter erosion, the dams to curtail rapids—all had the ephemeral lifespan of the six summer months, so great was the irreparable variability of those arteries.

Finally, immense high reservoirs were built, in steps down the Pyrenees, to store the flood waters. And they stored up disaster as well—in the collapse of walls and the resulting avalanche of rushing water that swept away entire towns.

But even if the rupture of the compensatory reservoirs had not come to constitute some of the most dramatic episodes in the history of engineering, even if those constructions had been able to hold firm and eliminate risk, we, no matter our effort and financial outlay, would not be able to build works the way the Purus itself has already built them for us.

In that regard, consider the following example. To give a consistent form to the Neste, a small river with an average discharge of twenty-five cubic meters, and thereby to minimize its flooding, Duparchel calculated the need for a reservoir that would hold 300 trillion liters of water—and then was overwhelmed by that colossal figure.

Now the Neste is one-third the size of the Yaco, which in turn is not considered even one of the major affluents of the Purus.

In the face of such formidable data, it becomes clear that the creation of compensatory reservoirs for that great river would amount to the construction of an ocean, and one must conclude that the numerous natural reservoirs that form along its course in fact represent a resource of inestimable value, one exceeding whatever is imaginable in development budgets.

We need at very least to preserve the Purus. Let us draw from a century-old lesson. The Mississippi, which in its lower stretches replicates the course of the Purus with the precision of a copy, was, for exactly the same reasons, even more clogged with impediments, thus almost impenetrable, and in many places completely unnavigable. Some of its tributaries were not merely shut off; they had literally disappeared under log jams.

Nevertheless, the great river, today transformed, stands as one of the most vibrant indexes of American persistence.

There is, however, within its valley—in one of its tributaries, the Red River—a discouraging case. It is a lost river. The Yankee was too late in discovering it. The huge underwater jam, dubbed "the great raft," which formed exactly like those that form in the Purus, extending its labyrinth of logs and dead branches for 630 kilometers. And there it is, indestructible, having over twenty-two years defied every effort to accomplish an impossible unclogging.

In light of the proportional relationship between that minuscule river and the Purus—and between us and the Americans—we can fairly well evaluate the difficulties lying in wait for us if the proliferation of the obstacles to which we have been referring continues—obstacles whose removal, along with basic protection of those banks most in danger of erosion, is at present relatively easy. Such measures will also lessen the aforementioned sudden "wanderings" that constitute a true anomaly in a river with the profile of stability we have seen demonstrable, even geometrically.

In any case, it is urgently important for us to initiate a modest but consistent program of improvements, to be passed down from federal government to federal government in a continuous, unbreakable commitment of honor with the future. Small at the outset but increasing with resource growth, such a program will be necessary in order to save the majestic river.

Somewhere, Von den Steinen, with that incomparably sharp wit of his, picturesquely called the Xingu the "stepchild" of our geography.

Let us carry the comparison out further.

If the Xingu is the stepchild, then the Purus is our "foundling."

We must incorporate it into our progress, within which it can in the final analysis be one of the major factors. For it is along that river's gigantic course that one of the boldest lines of our historical expansion is today taking place.

This Accursed Climate

The climatic definition of the territorial possessions created by the
Treaty of Petropolis has always included a curious element, in the
face of which the most pedestrian of psychiatrists supplants in com-
petency Professor Hann or any other master of meteorological science.
That element is the moral decline of the people who go there, even though
they may bring with them from the day of their departure the intent to
return to their place of origin as quickly as possible. A new class of exile
has been created: the exile who seeks exile, often striving to attain it
by eliminating competitors, while at the very same time building up in
his feverish fantasy the most doleful images in prefiguration of the
shadowy paradise that attracts him.

Such an exile sets out bearing in his very emotional state a susceptibility to all manner of illnesses.

He invests fifteen interminable days rounding our north coast. He
goes into the Amazon. He takes heart for a moment upon meeting
the singular physiognomy of the land. But then comes the low-lying
immensity—where his gaze is exhausted by the very scene he is contemplating, enormous to be sure but content-less, reduced to the vague
frame provided by distant banks. He travels up the great river. And the
days pass without definition before the strange motionlessness of a
picture done in one single color, one single height, and one single model,
to which is added the dread sensation that life has simply stopped. Every

impression is inert. The concept of time is abolished, for the succession of uniform external phenomena does not disclose it. This soul withdraws into a nostalgia that is the longing not merely for native land but for Land, for the natural forms traditionally linked to our contemplations. They are not available here—or do not stand out amid the uniformity of the plains.

He travels up one of the great tributaries: the Juruá or the Purus. He reaches his distant destination. All his forebodings intensify. The land is naturally graceless and sad because it is new. It just is. The forest lacks the artistic touches that human labor adds.

There are cultivated landscapes that we sometimes see subjectively, as a subconscious reflex of old, ancestral contemplations. Rolling hills, valleys, shorelines marked by inlets, and even dry deserts can present themselves to our eyes in such a way that we feel within ourselves some sort of atavistic reminiscence. When we first see them we feel the enchantment of relating what we imagine to what we would like, in an obvious externalization of previously idealized forms.

Here, such is simply not the case. The topographic forms most associated with human existence are absent. There is something unearthly about this amphibian nature, this mixture of land and water, that is hidden, completely at ground level, within its very grandeur. And one gets the sense that its impenetrability would go on forever did it not abound in precious products directly acquirable without the need for the constancy of cultivation. The people who live in the Amazon work it in the wild. They do not cultivate it, thereby making it attractive; they merely tame it. Those who come here—the Cearense, the Paraibano, the northern *sertanejo* in general—settle and carry out without knowing it one of the great undertakings of our time. They tame the wilderness. Rather than robust physiques, their simple souls, simultaneously ingenuous and heroic, disciplined by the adversities they encounter, are what guarantee them victory in this formidable campaign.

One recently arrived from the south comes upon this undertaking in tumultuous action and usually succumbs to it. He is overcome, shocked at one and the same time by the unfamiliar appearance of the countryside and that society of titanic *caboclos* who are busy building a territory here. He feels dislocated in space and in time; not outside his country but nonetheless estranged from human culture, lost in the hidden recesses of the forest and an obscure corner of history.

He cannot hold out. He focuses all the discipline he has left on the sole objective of staying for some time, useless and inert, at the post to which he has been assigned. Hardly performing even the simplest tasks, he follows with his eyes every steamboat going downstream. His spirit is off in his distant homeland, absorbed in an exhausting state of apprehension and conjecture. Then one stifling midday, a sudden, unexpected shiver of cold shakes him, signaling the liberatory onset—often secretly desired—of fever. It is a surprise most welcome. With that nudge from death as it passes by, life suddenly reawakens for him. Malaria means, above all else, a letter of emancipation in the form of medical certification. And return home. Return without fear, justifiable flight, legalized desertion, fear gilded over with heroism, defying the amazement of those who will hear him tell the alarming saga of the diseases that devastate this accursed land.

For it is necessary to rehabilitate departure. Then every nameless side channel, or *igarapé*, is a lugubrious, pestilent Ganges. And the *igapós* spread out over the soggy flatlands like numberless Pontine marshes. A frightening and tragic retrospective picture is drawn out in an imaginative recitation of sorrows. And day after day the nature accursed by that man keeps reappearing in that place before misled imaginations, as though in it the classical locus of misery and death were being staked out.

The exaggeration is obvious. The Acre—or, in general, the Amazonian plain divided down the middle by the long course of the Purus— probably has the lethality common to all areas recently opened to settlement. But the incidence is relatively low.

A quick comparison demonstrates as much.

The schools of colonial medicine in England and France have taught us, merely in their titles, the safeguards that should attend the transplantation of people to new habitats. A patent of nobility exists in modern expansionist imperialism, which serves to absolve it of the greatest crimes, namely, that its brilliant generals are transformed into anonymous scouting parties of physicians and engineers; the greatest battles merely recall the greater campaign, the campaign against the climate; and domination of the inferior races is the beginning of the redemption of territories in a magnificent sweep that holds out to all parts of the globe the marvelous undertaking of the hygienification of the land, from Tonkin to India, to Egypt, to Tunisia, to the Sudan, to the island of Cuba and to the Philippines.

Hygienification of the land and hygienification of man. The task is twofold. The calm conquerors are not satisfied with seeking out the meteorological or telluric causes of the diseases present in the newly conquered areas, diseases that run on an indeterminate scale from summer anemias to polymorphous fevers. They also take on the greater burden of shaping new organisms for new environments, correcting temperaments and destroying old inflexible habits or creating new ones until, through a process both compensatory and stimulative, they build a totally acclimated individual, one often so transformed in physical and psychic features that he is truly an artificial native created by hygiene. Therefore the settler or the emigrant has everywhere become a pupil of the state. From the day of his departure, itself preestablished at the most propitious time of year, his every act, down to the last detail of dress and sustenance, are predetermined by exacting regulations. Within the general range of the features of the hot climate to which he is moving, the structure of an individual hygiene is designed for him, in which all accidents are foreseen—even dangers to organic stability inevitable in the physiological phase of adaptation to a climatic environment whose depressive effect on the European runs from the musculature, which loses mass, to strength of spirit, which weakens. Thus prophylactic measures, which begin to suggest themselves in the study of the physical factors, not infrequently end up being extended to form a beautiful code of practical morality. Along with the common precepts designed to inure man to the high temperatures and excessive humidity that seek to depress blood pressure and activity, close the safety valves that are the pores, fatigue the heart and the nerves—in short, to create in him a morbid susceptibility to the ills that develop from the malaria that continuously undermines his very life and the dermatoses that devastate his skin— what stand out as most efficacious and decisive are those that prepare him to resist despair, the melancholy of a monotonous and primitive existence, the increasing bitterness of loneliness, the irritability derived from the intensely bright and electrified air, the isolation. And above all else the breakdown of the will into a sudden and profound spiritual decline that would seem to be the unique illness of these climes, from which all the others spring as though they were symptoms of it and it alone.

Open any regulation book of colonial hygiene. What stands out even to a cursory reading are the incomparable efforts of modern colonization and its complex mission which, in complete contrast to that of its predecessors, do not contemplate introducing the transformed barbarians to civilization but rather transplanting civilization integrally to the primitive and adverse barbarian territories themselves.

In the pages of any of those books what sometimes strikes us more than the prodigies of prescience and of knowledge developed to adapt the outlander to the environment is the excessively slow course of application, not to mention the failure of their most resolute efforts.

France in Indochina, with an almost temperate climate, has invested fifteen years of continuous work in an effort to lower mortality rates. Acquiescing to the opinions of their best scientists, after many trials it has rejected systematic settlement of equatorial Africa. The same has occurred in general in English, German, and Belgian colonies. It is sufficient to note that their official agents have an assignment rotation of no longer than three years. Return to the native land is an indispensable security measure to restore weakened organisms. In this way, despite great investment and sacrifice and the prodigies of sanitation engineering, which have transformed the topographical primitiveness of the new lands, constituting a veritable scientific geography, what in the last analysis is created in them are precarious societies made up of perpetual convalescents linked to inflexible diets and surviving by dint of the intolerable formulas of complex pharmacopeias.

Now, comparing these colonizing projects constrained within the precepts of rigorous statutes (and with so little result to show) to our haphazard colonization, our hands-off settlement of the Acre (which has produced surprising results), one does not have to adduce arguments to support the proposition that the conditions in that supposedly accursed region are not only superior to that of the majority of the areas recently opened to colonial expansion but also superior to those of a great many normally inhabited countries.

In fact—leaving aside the positive factor that the settlers were already accustomed to the latitude—History knows no more striking example of an emigration at one and the same time so anarchic, sudden, and contrary to the most basic precepts of acclimatization as the one that, from 1879 down to today, has hurled successive waves of our *sertanejo* population from the territory between Paraíba and Ceará upon that corner of the Amazon. Even a cursory glance shows that from its beginnings it was carried out lacking not only the slow, progressive pace of careful migration but also the most basic administrative oversight.

The settlement of the Acre is an entirely fortuitous historical case, one outside the basic lines of our progress.

It has its dark underside, of which no one is unaware: the periodic droughts in our northern backlands, which generate the periodic mass exodus of afflicted multitudes. That exodus is not a response to a crisis of growth and the creation of an overabundance capable of energizing other areas, expanding into itineraries that are the visible diagram of the triumphal march of the races. It is rather determined by scarcity of life opportunity and complete defeat in the face of natural calamity. Its lines jumble together within a chaotic pattern of flight. And an inverted natural selection has aggravated it: all the weak, all the useless, all the diseased, and all the sacrificed dispatched randomly, like the leftovers of the race, into the wilderness. When the great droughts of 1879–1880, 1889–1890, 1900–1901 scourged the arid *sertões* and in a few weeks the coastal cities filled with a population of refugees, starving, overcome with fever and smallpox, the single concern of the public powers consisted of liberating the cities as soon as possible from that invasion of moribund barbarians infesting Brazil. Steamboats were quickly crammed full of those troublesome cargoes consigned to death. They were sent to the Amazon—vast, unpopulated, almost unknown—which amounted to expatriating them within their own country. That martyred multitude, all rights lost, family ties severed, torn apart in the tumult of forced departure, in effect set out bearing sealed marching orders to the unknown. And it went with its starving, its fever victims, and its pox infected, in conditions that would contaminate and corrupt the healthiest locales in the world. And once this purgative task was performed, no further attention was paid. Government intervention ceased. Never, down to our own days, has a single government agent, or doctor, been involved in the case. The banished bore with them the single, sorrowful mission of simply disappearing.

But they did not disappear. On the contrary, in less than thirty years the area that was a vague geographical term, a swampy wilderness stretching out limitlessly to the southwest, has suddenly defined itself, contributing substantially to our economic development.

Its capital—a city ten years of age set upon the site of two centuries of abandoned efforts at settlement—has transformed itself into the metropolis of the most navigable river in South America. And in that almost mysterious extreme southwest of the Amazon, where a remarkable man, William Chandless, traveled 3,200 kilometers without finding the river's origins, 100,000 *sertanejos*—resurrected souls—unexpectedly appeared and repatriated themselves in a heroic and original manner: they have extended national reach into the new areas that they themselves opened up.

Page through the most recent reports from the prefectures in the Acre. What astonishes in them more than the unmatched transformations taking place there is the absolute casualness, the complete calm, with which settlement is being carried out. Today, just as thirty years ago, despite the problems and the upheaval of the droughts, the immigrants are advancing without even minimal support and without official assistance.

The transplanted populations establish themselves nonetheless, putting down roots in the land. The demographic progress is astonishing. And now there stretches from the headwaters of the Juruá to the confluence of the Abunã the increasingly sought after promised land of northern Brazil.

The contrast is revealing. The reputation that a climate such as this has for unhealthiness repeats a misunderstanding. What has taken place and is still taking place—albeit on a lesser scale in the Acre—is "telluric selection" as Kirchoff speaks of it: a kind of natural examination, or judicial review carried out by nature on those individuals who have come into its domain, by which it reserves the right to exist for only those whom it chooses to favor.

But the process is a general one.

In all latitudes the elective affinity between land and man has always been pivotal at the outset. Those who have best balanced climatic factors and personal attributes are the ones who survived. The best acclimatization derives from the binary combination of physical and moral strengths that, on the one hand, range from those that relate to the most basic elements of sense data—thermic, hygrometric, or barometric—to the most subjective impressions arising from aspects of the countryside; on the other hand, it derives as well from features ranging from vital cell resistance or muscle tone to the more complex and refined energies of character. In early stages, before the hereditary transmission of the acquired characteristics of resistance can guarantee the status of individuals within the adaptation of the race itself, inevitable, even necessary, lethality merely reveals the effects of a selection process. All acclimatization is thus a permanent plebiscite in which the newcomer is chosen for survival. In the tropics it is natural that biological scrutiny should have a central role.

There are no tricks that can be employed to avoid this scrutiny. Its incorruptible process falls equally on the tubercular, incapable of full respiratory activity in the caustic, oxygen-poor air and the lascivious wanton; the victim of heart disease, reduced by loss of blood pressure, and the alcoholic, arrogant candidate for every disease that comes along; the lymphatic, suddenly taken by anemia, and the glutton; the sleepwalker, weakened by his nightly vigils, and the slothful, stagnated in enervating siestas; and the choleric, the neurasthenic with nerves resonating uncontrollably in the electrically charged air under the mysterious influence of the dazzling firmament, all the way to paroxysms of tropical dementia, which strike him down like a sort of mental sunstroke.

For every physiological or moral false step there is a corresponding corrective of physical reaction. What is called unhealthiness is in fact a purification, the generalized elimination of the unfit. In fine, it sometimes becomes clear that it is not the climate that is bad; it is the man.

That is in great part what happened in the Acre. The populating levies that came to that area—with no examination of who they contained and under deplorable transportation conditions—also came face-to-face with a social situation that further aggravated their weaknesses and instability.

What awaited them—and still awaits them, albeit on a lesser scale—is the most imperfect organization of labor that human egotism has ever devised.

Let me repeat. The emigrant *sertanejo* has created here an anomaly that cannot be overemphasized: he is the man who toils in order to enslave himself.

While the Italian settler might move from Genoa to the most remote farm in São Paulo, paternally assisted by our public agencies, the Cearense realizes, at his own expense and unsupported in any way, a much more difficult journey, in which the advances made by the insatiable contractors, bloated with unheard of prices and fantastic returns, more often than not transform him into a perpetually insolvent debtor.

From the first hatchet blow, his own activity ensnares him in an unbearable, vicious circle: exhaustive labor in the effort to pay off a debt that, menacingly, continues to grow and grow in such a way as to parallel the very toils and efforts that would discharge it.

He is completely alone in his dolorous labor. The harvesting of *seringa*—in this respect worse that the gathering of its competitor, *caucho* —is carried out in isolation. There is a Siberian element to this labor. Dostoyevsky could make his more lugubrious chapters even grimmer with this torture: man constrained to tread the same "path" for his entire life. It is a path on which he is the only traveler, a darkling, narrow, winding path that intermittently and maddeningly takes him back to the same point of departure. He is trapped in that Sisyphean undertaking, pushing his own body instead of a boulder—starting out, coming back to the beginning, and then starting out again—in the crushing toils of a demonic circle, the eternal round of someone locked up in a prison without walls. All this aggravated by the exercise of a rudimentary job, one that he can learn in an hour and performs for his whole life—automatically, in simple reflex motions. If he is not fortified with a solid moral structure, with his intelligence atrophied he will lose the hope, the ingenuous illusions, and the reinforcing enthusiasm that brought him to this pass, to this adventure, in the search of fortune.

In exact parallel comes organic decline.

Year after year, he is deprived of nutrition, which is the solidest base of tropical hygiene, for he does not engage in even the most rudimentary cultivation to provide himself with it. Indeed, in contradiction of all precept, his diet is limited to various kinds of suspect and harmful canned goods supplemented by meat according to the luck of the hunt.

Above all else is abandonment. The *seringueiro* is necessarily a solitary figure.

Even in the Acre proper, where the greater density of rubber trees permits the opening of sixteen sections, or "paths," per square league, that area—capable, according to the current calculation of the agricultural unit, of supporting the families of fifty subsistence farmers— requires the labor of only eight *seringueiros* spread out over the terrain, rarely catching sight of one another. If we calculate an average rubber tract as having two hundred such paths, it will cover nearly fifteen square leagues. And that latifundium, which could be populated with up to three thousand active inhabitants, holds no more than the invisible population of one hundred exaggeratedly dispersed workers.

This is the systematic preservation of the wilderness—and the cellular imprisonment of man—upon the open face of the land.

In the face of these basic lineaments of so anomalous a social picture, the question about the lethality of the Acre recedes. What stands out undeniably is the concept that there is a healthiness supportive of that number of beings submitted to so imperfect a regimen. It is even believed that the characteristics of the tropical, which are limited to the lower latitudes, from eight to eleven degrees, which demarcate that region, are merely theoretical and that, taking into proper account the moderating influence doubtless exercised by the overwhelming mass of the forest that both covers and encircles the region, one can conclude that further meteorological observation, barely begun today, may revise the twenty-five-degree isotherm that has been assigned to it, without basis, on the maps.

Because, the erroneousness and viciousness of the settlement process and life in the region aside, recently arrived society is acclimating itself and making progress.

Even the most incurious traveler who observes the Purus cannot help but notice the slow, continual transformation.

The early explorer is slowly adjusting to the land on which he walked indifferently for a considerable time. He now clears a place on which to locate his hut. And the first agricultural sites are now to be seen, laid out on the beaches that are revealed at low water, or on the *firmes*, above flood level. The shabby *barracões* covered with palm leaves have given way to regular dwellings or large estate houses, built of stone and mortar. Sebastopol, Canacori, São Luís de Cassianã, Itatuba, Realeza, and scores of other locations in the Lower Purus, along with Liberdade and Concórdia farther up, have expanded into veritable villages with numerous dwellings often sited on roads next to small churches. They are the material image of dominion and definitive possession.

In this sense, the evolution is tangible.

Even the original names, some of them outlandish but all of them eloquent, of the settlements from the oldest to the most recent times, bespeak as much. In the land without history the first facts are written, scattered and fragmentary, in place names. First comes the initial, torturous phase of adaptation, which evokes sadness, martyrdom, even cries of despair or calls for help. The traveler reads on the large signboards on the sides of the houses turned out to the river: "God Save Us," "Homesickess," "Saint John of the Misery," "Hidden," "Hell" . . . Then the strong rebirth of hope and overflowing good humor of a people redeemed: "Good Beginning," "New Enchantment," "I Want to See!" "Liberty," "Concord," "Paradise."

As one goes up the river the rebirth becomes more pronounced. In various stretches after the confluence with the Acre one travels among dwellings that face each other or line up along the shore, as though one were traversing a highly developed region long since opened up. No longer the shabbiness and roughness of the earlier makeshift dwellings.

In such settlements as Catiana and Macapá, as in the rest upstream all the way to the last, Sobral, with its tiny coffee plantation that supplies local consumption, one sees in every aspect, from the widespread local cultivation to the well-tended orchards, the caring labor of the settler, who beautifies the land not to abandon it.

And the men are admirable.

I have seen them up close. Let us converse with them.

I shall retain their bizarre names, from the prosperous "Caboclo Real" of Cachoeira to the garrulous "Cai n'Água" from the region around the Chandless; from old "João Amarelo" who founded Cataí and still unfailingly brings his seventy years of hard labor down the long, winding road of the paths; to the fearless Antônio Dourado of Terra Alta, unerring rifle shot, whose deeds of bravery in the skirmishes with the *caucheros* in 1903 constitute a vibrant page of derring-do.

Looking at them, reviewing the organic integrity that reveals itself in their solid musculature or the moral beauty of the manly souls that conquered the wilderness and bearing in mind the horrible conditions that they encountered in the early days—or that they still encounter, albeit lessened—one finds oneself at a loss to explain their vigorous existences under so malign and brutal a climatological regimen as characterizes the Acre.

Nor does the argument hold weight that the northern *sertanejo*, or more precisely, the *jagunço*—beyond the advantage of having to move only more or less laterally on the globe—came endowed with the pastoral and warlike abstinence of the Arab and thus previously prepared for the new habitat by the inexorable discipline of the droughts.

The Purus and the Juruá have long been open destinations for a motley array of foreigners: the Syrian, arrived directly from Beirut, who has slowly supplanted the Portuguese as the river trader; the adventurous, artistic Italian who spends long months traveling the rivers with photographic equipment collecting the most typical faces of the Indians of the forest and scenes of the wild countryside; the impassive Saxon, having traded his native mists for the splendors of the equatorial air. In the vast majority they all thrive there, carry out their activities, prosper, and live long lives.

Let us register one particular case. In 1872 Barrington Brown and William Lidstone traveled through the Lower Purus to Huitanaã, setting out in the launch Guajará commanded by a Captain Hoefner, "a German speaking both English and Portuguese," as the two travelers explain in the interesting book that they wrote.[1]

That was thirty-five years ago.

Captain Hoefner is still there, eternal launch commander, plying his trade tirelessly upon the same accursed waters, in which sucking buffalo gnats teem, along with mosquitoes, emissaries of fever, and bobbing *mururé* water lilies spread out, floating in concert with the imperceptible current—with violet flowers that recall sad burial garlands. Amid it all, the German has gone on without wavering.

I saw him at the end of 1905 at the confluence of the Acre. He is a lively, active old man, hardworking and diligent, with an open, rosy face framed with completely white hair. If he were on the streets of Berlin, the somber stigma of the tropics would hardly be noticed on his lightly bronzed complexion.

Cases of this type abound, each a comment contributing to the extinction of a myth.

One last argument perhaps remains, given the persistence with which it is made. It is that those sturdy *caboclos* and that exceptional Saxon are not products of the environment; that they come in spite of the environment; that they have been victorious in a battle to the death in which those who were not endowed with the same characteristics of strength, energy, and abstinence succumbed in great numbers.

If such is the case, then let us put sterile sentimentalism aside once and for all and admit that it is the climate that performs the superior function. In the face of the harmful circumstances that occasioned and motivated the populating of the Acre—long years open to the entry of all kinds of disease and all of the vices enabled by the indifference of public authority—it has exercised an incorruptible review, liberating that territory from calamities and abuses that might well have grown beyond all proportion, much greater than those to be observed there today.

It has policed, it has cleansed, it has moralized. It has selected—and continues to select—the most worthy for life. It has eliminated—and continues to eliminate—the less fit, through flight or through death.

It is a climate to be admired that prepares new regions for the strong, for the steadfast, and for the good.

NOTE

1. Charles Barrington Brown and William Lidstone, *Fifteen Thousand Miles in the Amazon and Its Tributaries* (London, 1878).

The Caucheros

Some fifty years ago, east of the right bank of the Ucayali and of the rolling hills within which the Javari, the Juruá, and the Purus have their sources, a new society came into being. It took shape quietly. Hidden away in the depths of the jungle, it was familiar only to a few traders from Pará, in whose businesses there began to arrive from that remote origin the dark gray slabs of another elastic gum that would compete with *seringa* for the industrial market.

The substance was *caucho*. And the adventurous backlanders who ventured fearlessly into those unknown reaches soon came to be called *caucheros*.

They came from the west, across the Andes, braving the whole gamut of the earth's climates, from the hot Pacific coasts to the frozen mountain highlands. Between them and their native region stood two six-thousand-meter walls and a long ditch filled with ravines. Before them, the Amazonian flatlands: an expanse of hundreds of miles leading endlessly northeast, eventually disappearing into the Atlantic without the aid of a hill to cast its immensity in any relief whatsoever.

Never has so imposing a backdrop set the scene for such small actors.

It is natural for those frontiersmen to have journeyed long years alone, unnoticed, invisible, moving carefully in the perpetual twilight of these distant forests. For here difficulties more serious than the enormous distances and the dangers of the wilderness slowed their already cautious steps.

In fact, the entire area where the Peru–Brazil border is drawn—albeit still with a dotted line—an area from which the beginnings of the Purus and the Juruá, the northernmost sources of the Urubamba and the remotest forks of the Madre de Dios all spread out in their respective directions, figures as one of the least known on the American continent. This is the case not because of exceptional physical conditions, for the area was conquered in 1844 by Francis Castelnau, but because of the frightening reputation of the tribes that people it. Under the generic name *chunchos*, they have become the greatest fear of even the most daring of explorers.

The tribes are countless. Anyone going up the Purus and observing, in the area around Cachoeira, the Paumaris, ever decreasing in number and hardly recalling the old masters of those lands, or, further upstream, the peaceful Ipurinás, or, even past the Yaco, the Tacunas, born looking old, so much is the decrepitude of their race reflected in their stunted aspect, will be surprised when he comes face-to-face with the singular savages who populate the headwaters. With all their varied origins and customs, they are concentrated here in forced proximity. The gentle Amauacas who congregate around the *puestos*, or outposts, of the *caucho* harvesters. The indomitable Coronauas, masters of the headwaters of the Curanja. The bronzed Piros, with shiny teeth stained with a dark resin that give their faces an indefinable aspect of grave threat when they smile. The bearded Caxibos, inured to extermination after two hundred years of attacks against the remains of the Pachitea missions. The Conibos, with deformed craniums and chests frighteningly striped red and blue. The Setebos, the Sipibos, the Iurimanas. The corpulent Mashcos of the Manú, recalling in their great size the giants imagined by the first cartographers of the Amazon region. And above all others, supplanting them in valor and renown, the warlike Campas of the Urubamba.

The number of different nations in so small an area bespeaks the unusual pressure that bears upon them. Their concentration is a forced one.

They obviously find themselves in the last redoubt, having retreated here at the end of a century-long campaign against them, which dates from the Maynas missions to the modern expeditions and whose culminating episodes have been lost to History.

The contemporary narrator arrives during the final act of a drama and sees, astonished, only the close of the last scene.

Civilization, barbarously armed with its lethal rifles, besieges the cornered savage. The Peruvians from the west and the south; the Brazilians in the entire northeastern sector; and on the southeast the Bolivians, shutting off access to the Madre de Dios valley.

The *caucheros* appear as the most advantaged intruders in this sinister catechism of fire and sword that, off in this remote backland, continues to exterminate the most interesting native peoples of South America.

This historic mission has fallen to them because of the fragility of a tree. The *cauchero* is necessarily a nomad sworn to combat, destruction, and a wandering or tumultuous life, because the elastic *Castilloa* that is the source of the raw latex he seeks does not admit of stable exploitation like the Brazilian *Hevea*, which regularly produces the liquid that is tapped from it. The *Castilloa* is exceptionally fragile. Cut open, it dies, or withers uselessly for a prolonged period of time. Therefore the harvester simply cuts it down and harvests it completely. He makes cuts in the fallen tree at meter intervals, from the prop roots to the smallest leaf-bearing branches. After digging out shallow cavities in the ground below each cut, he leaves and returns the next week to collect from the cavities the precious strips of *caucho*. What remains stuck to the bark, around the edges of the cuts, or scattered randomly on the ground is gathered up to make the less valuable *sernambi*.

The process is rudimentary and quick. Even the densest of *caucho* groves is soon exhausted. And since *Castilloas* are not regularly distributed through the forest but grow in widely separated groves, the harvesters move from place to place, replicating without variation all the comings and goings of the aleatory life of tree hunters.

In this sense, a nomadic life is imposed on them. It is the inviolable condition for their success. They bravely penetrate the wilderness, they congregate at one remote site after another, and they never return to the path previously taken. Condemned to the unknown, they adapt to a life of new and forbidding places. They get there. They leave. They go on their way. Never do they establish a connection with the arduously conquered locales.

Reaching a site where *caucho* has been discovered, they raise a first palm leaf hut called a *tambo* at the top of a slope and immediately throw themselves into their laborious task. Their principal work implements are a Winchester carbine (the short rifle handily deployed in skirmishes amid the thickly entwined foliage), a sharp machete, which they use to clear away the tangles of vine, and a portable compass to orient them along the jumbled trails. These in hand, they set out to reconnoiter the surrounding area. They go to ascertain the whereabouts of the savage, with whom they must struggle and whom they must exterminate or enslave in order to secure their new place of work and to summon the many strong backs necessary to carry it out.

This requisite and frightening first step is not infrequently carried out by only a few. A half dozen men, each in his own direction, silently penetrating the dense jungle. They move along, peering into every recess, keeping their ears tuned, covering, foot by foot, all the likely hiding places; keeping track of unusual features by heart, in an exhaustive topographical inventory. At the same time, with eyes and ears alert for the slightest sign or the faintest sound on the murmuring forest air, they remain on guard with all the resources and techniques demanded by this astonishing duel to the death with the wilderness.

Some never return. Others, after an uneventful scrutiny, come back safe and sound to their shelters. One, however, after exhaustive scouting, may glimpse in the distance, half hidden among the foliage, the outlying huts of a group of the savages.

He barely stifles a shout of triumph, and he does not rush away to tell his companions what he has discovered.

He distills his extraordinary abilities. He stays low to the ground and, crawling forward, "sniffing out danger," he gets as close as he can to the unsuspecting enemy.

In this act there is a moving aspect of heroism. Man, absolutely alone, seeks out the savage, his only escort the eighteen bullets loaded in his rifle.

It is a long, slow, tortuous creep in which he takes advantage of every possible piece of cover, hiding behind every tree trunk or in the angles of prop roots, gliding silently over the layers of decomposing branches, or winding his way among the intertwined stems of the banana trees with their large protective leaves—until, at the end of his agonizing, silent approach, he can see and hear the unsuspecting adversaries from up close, almost at the border of the open clearing, as they go on unaware of the sinister civilized intruder spying on them: counting their numbers, observing their manner, and evaluating their resources. After that exacting surveillance he goes back, bringing to his waiting companions all the information necessary for the conquest.

"Conquest" is the preferred term, used in a kind of atavistic reminiscence of the attacks engaged in long ago by Pizarro's mercenaries. But it is not effected by arms until rudimentary diplomacy in the form of gifts of the sort most desired by the savage has been exhausted. On a certain occasion I heard one man describe the following process. "We attract them to the *tambo* with gifts: clothing, rifles, machetes, etc. And without making them work we allow them to go back to their camp to tell their companions how they have been treated by the *caucheros*, who do not force them to work but instead merely advise them to work a little as they choose in order to pay for the presents they were given."

These peaceful means, however, generally fail. Then the rule is quarterless hunt with firearms. This is the heroic aspect of the undertaking: a small group daring to engage in the hunt of a much greater number.

About those episodes no details are given.

They come down to one constant tactic: the fastest shooting possible and maximum daring. Those are the guarantees of victory. This wilderness has seen an incalculable number of small battles in which tiny but well-armed groups have overthrown entire tribes, abruptly sacrificed because of the primitiveness of their arms and by their own valor in mounting head-on attacks against the repeating fire of carbines.

For example, when Carlos Fitzcarrald arrived at the headwaters of the Madre de Dios in 1892, having come from the Ucayali along the portage opened across the isthmus that now bears his name, he tried to find the best way possible to capture the Mashcos, who controlled that area. He brought with him, among the conquered Piros, an intelligent, loyal interpreter. He was able to see and talk with the chieftain of the savages.

The discussion was short and extremely curious.

After introducing the resources he had at his disposal and his small army, in which were mixed the discrete physiognomies of the tribes that he had subjugated, the renowned explorer attempted to demonstrate to the "infidel" the advantages of the alliance he was being offered, in contrast to the perils that would attend a disastrous battle. The Mashco's only response was to ask about the arrows Fitzcarrald brought with him. And Fitzcarrald, smiling, handed him a Winchester cartridge.

The savage looked it over for a long while, absorbed with the smallness of the projectile. He tried in vain to wound himself, pushing the bullet hard against his chest. Not achieving what he desired, he took up one of his own arrows and plunged it dramatically into his other arm.

He then smiled, indifferent to the pain, contemplating with pride his own blood as it squirted out . . . and without saying a word turned around and, leaving the astonished explorer standing there, went back to his encampment with an illusion of superiority that would soon be dashed. In fact, a half an hour later, around one hundred Mashcos, the naive and recalcitrant chief among them, lay slaughtered at the river's edge. Still today that place is called Mashcos Beach in remembrance of that bloody episode.

Thus is the wild region made safe. With the surroundings cleaned up, the natives within a few leagues' radius either killed or enslaved, the *caucheros* throw themselves feverishly into their arduous task. Within a few months, other *tambos* spring up alongside the first one. A solitary hut evolves into a large central building or noisy embarcadero. More and more buildings are added to produce little settlements like Cocama and Curanja on the banks of the Purus, and suddenly the wilderness projects the image of progress, albeit one that bursts forth, develops, and ends, all within a decade. The *caucheros* stay in such places until the last *Castilloa* falls. They come, they destroy, and then they move on. They seek nothing in the land and leave behind only a few small yucca and banana plantations tended by domesticated Indians. The only regular agriculture on the Upper Purus beyond where our *seringueiros* reach, limited though it is, is cotton growing by reservation Campas, which even in that activity seek Indian independence: picking, carding, spinning, weaving, and dying the *cushmas* they wear, which hang down from their shoulders to their feet like long, awkward togas. Thus amid the civilized foreigners who show up in the region for the purpose of wounding or killing man and tree, staying in one place only for the length of time necessary to extinguish both, and then moving on to other locations where they create the same confusion again, passing like a wave of destruction and leaving the savages even more savage, those singular barbarians manifest the only touch of stable society. The contrast is fascinating. Traveling from the Campa settlement of Tingoleales to the Peruvian site of Shamboyaco near the mouth of the Manuel Urbano River, the traveler does not, as at first he might believe, pass from more primitive to more elevated stages of human evolution. Instead he receives a surprise: he goes from outright barbarism to a kind of enfeebled civilization in which the defects of barbarism are more incisively evident within the very conquests of progress.

He reaches the Peruvian station, and in the first hours the atmosphere of noisy and animated existence fascinates him. The main living quarters and the buildings subordinate to it, some of them located along roads in the manner of small villages, are always constructed on a well-chosen site above flood level. And even though they are constructed exclusively out of the leaves and trunks of the *paxiúba*—the providential palm tree of the Amazon—they generally have two stories and in their elegance of line and in the sweeping verandahs that surround them present an appearance completely opposite to the dull *barracões* of our *seringueiros*.

On the ample open space ending at the crest of the river bank, which then falls in a sharp incline down to the river, a lively, happy bustle. Powerful loaders, moving in long lines, bending under the weight of slabs of *caucho*; active overseers rushing through the ground-floor doors and racing one way or another—to the warehouses fully stocked with canned goods or to the outbuildings where fire flashes and hammers and anvils screech as axes and machetes are repaired.

Below at the embarcadero teeming with quick dugouts, where the long paddles slice through the air, the hubub made by workers and boatmen echoes, and the rafts made exclusively of *caucho* bob low in the water—"merchandise that bears its bearers along with it" in formation upon the "moving roadway." And amid all this activity up and down the slope, the red skirts and white bodices of the gracious *cholas* of Iquitos, passing and weaving their way along in a festive panoply.

The traveler passes these groups in motion, and the surprises do not cease. He climbs the stairs that lead to the front verandah, onto which the dwelling's main rooms open. At the top the *cauchero*—an ostentatious and jovial man standing tall on the sturdy heels of his bush boots—receives him effusively, opening each of the double doors in a bluff and grand hospitality. The spell is carried out to its completion. Separated from the concept of time, or that of the great space of thousands of kilometers spent plying lonely rivers to reach this remote outpost, the outsider unconsciously imagines himself in a commercial entrepôt in any of the coastal cities. There is nothing that does not support the illusion: the long pine counter that divides the main room and bars access to the company space where shelves can be seen stacked with merchandise; the obsequious employees, obedient to the orders of the hypercorrect bookkeeper who had greeted him as he entered and then went back to his accounts, bending over his sloping desk; the glass of beer offered him instead of the traditional *chicha*; the picture calendar on one wall marking the correct day of the year; the newspapers from Manaus and Lima; and even—shockingly—the refined and elegant torture of a phonograph, scratching out, in this corner of the wilderness, a favorite aria by a famous tenor.

But all these astonishing appearances vanish before a scrutiny that permits the visitor to see what his well-presented host does not disclose. Then disillusionment assaults him, and it is decisive. The image of superior life does not reach beyond the small piece of land, less than a hectare, located between the menacing bush close behind and the bank sloping down to the river.

Beyond this false scenario the real drama that takes place is all but inconceivable for our time.

Below the well-off *cauchero*, on a lamentable scale that runs from the mestizo come here from Loreto seeking his fortune to the depressed Quichua brought down from the mountains, comes an unending series of the victimized. To see them one must penetrate the dark recesses of the trackless forest and approach the solitary huts where they dwell totally alone, accompanied only by their inseparable rifle, which guarantees their survival through the chance resource of hunted game. Here they labor long years to little avail; here they become ill, devoured by disease; here they die in absolute abandonment. Often as many as four hundred men whom no one sees, scattered across this terrain, appearing only once in a great while at the straw castle of the haughty baron who enslaves them. The "conquerer" does not keep track of them. He knows that they will not run away. All around for a radius of six leagues, which is his full domain, the region, full of savages, is impenetrable. The wilderness itself is a perpetually vigilant overseer. It guards his numerous slave holdings for him. Even the proud *Campas*, whom he captured by practicing a magisterial perfidy against the barbarian's ingenuous bravery, will not dare leave him, fearing their own wild brothers, who will never pardon them for their transitory subjugation.

Thus the happy adventurer who two years earlier in Lima or Arequipa had exercised a gentler style has come to feel completely free from the pressures of society and the infinite social correctives. Having acquired a sense of unchecked dominion and at the same time a sense of impunity for all caprices and crimes, he quickly descends to a highly original form of savagery—without losing the superior attributes of the milieu in which he was born.

The *cauchero* is in fact not just a completely new character in History; he is, above all else, antinomic and paradoxical. Even the most detailed ethnographic table has no space for him. At first glance he would seem to represent the common case of a civilized man gone native, in a terrifying backslide in which civilized characteristics are erased by primitive forms of activity.

But that would be a mistake. He does not combine those counterposed states to create a stable, defined activity that might be termed "hybrid." He merely puts them side by side; he does not mix them together. His is a case of psychic mimetism: a man who pretends to be a savage in order to defeat the savage. He is gentleman and wild man according to circumstance. The curious dualism of one who seeks to keep the best moral teaching intact alongside a morality fashioned specifically for the wilderness shows through in all the acts of his turbulent existence. The same man who with enviable rectitude strives to meet his commitments, which often add up to millions upon millions of reis, with the exporters of Iquitos or Manaus, does not hesitate to cheat the lowly *peón* who serves him over a few kilos of common *sernambi*.[1] Or he may go directly from the most refined gallantry to the greatest brutality, leaving in between a captivating smile and impeccable manners; his gleaming knife in hand, he charges, with a bellow, the disobedient *cholo* who dares cross him.

The savagery is a mask that he can put on and take off at will.

His is not to be likened to the incomparable figure of the *bandeirante*, our colonial conquistador. Antônio Raposo, for example, stands out among all South American conquerers. His heroism was brutal and massive: no quarter, no pretense, no hesitation. He advanced unintelligently, mechanically, inflexibly, like a force of nature unleashed. The 1,500-league diagonal line that he cut through the heart of South America from São Paulo to the Pacific, over rivers, high plains, swamps, stagnant backwaters, deserts, mountains, snow-covered wildernesses and harsh coastlines, amid the fear and the ruin of a hundred extirpated tribes, was a fearsome deed of epic proportions. But one can clearly sense in that individual daring the marvelous concentration of all the acts of daring of an entire era.

The *bandeirante* was brutal, inexorable, but logical.

He was the superman of the wilderness.

The *cauchero*, by contrast, is irritatingly absurd in his elegant brutality, in his bloody gallantry, and in his sometimes heroism. He is the homunculus of civilization.

But understand this counterpoint. That adventurer goes into the wilderness with the exclusive goal of getting rich and going back. Going back as soon as possible, fleeing that swampy, melancholy land that does not seem to possess the solidity to sustain the very material weight of a society. During all of the conjunctures of his agitated and feverish activity he has in his mind the spectacle of vast cities where one day, with the "black gold" of *caucho* converted into pounds sterling, he will stand out. Thoroughly dominated by an incurable nostalgia for the native milieu that he left precisely and only for the purpose of returning supplied with the resources to provide him with a greater quotient of happiness, he hurls himself upon the forests: he subjugates and domesticates the savages; he resists malaria and exhaustion; he strives madly for four, five, six years; he accumulates some hundreds of thousands of soles, and then suddenly he disappears.

He turns up in Paris. He lives, in the full splendor of noisy theaters and salons, six months of delirious life with no one discovering the slightest hint of his professional nomadism in anything that might belie the correctness of his dress and his manners. He bankrupts himself in brilliant style. And then he returns . . . he takes up his old routine where he left it. A new four to six years of forced work; a new quick fortune made; another jump across the ocean; and almost always another anxious return in search of the easily lost fortune, in a stupendous oscillation between the bright avenues and the solitary forest.

The most amazing stories circulate in this regard, in which famous *caucheros* well known in Manaus play principal roles.

In that life of oscillation he puts a provisional character into everything he does in this land that he detests and devastates—from the house he builds in ten days to last five years to intimate relationships that sometimes last years only to have him undo them in a day. On this point especially he can be seen to practice an unrivaled inconstancy. One such man, on being asked in Curanja where he had wed the gentle Amauaca who had accompanied him for ten years with the care of an exemplary spouse, answered us, slightly ironically: "She was a gift given me in Pachitea."

A "gift," a present, an expendable object that he would unconcernedly discard at the first eventuality.

The aforementioned owner of that run-down little settlement, who in Lima or Iquitos would be a perfect model of the peaceful and abstemious bourgeois, here "hungry for women," introduces to friend and chance visitor alike his scandalous harem, which includes the fascinating Mercedes, she of the "doe eyes," who cost a battle with the Coronauas, and the enchanting Facunda with huge, savage, and dreamy eyes, who cost him 100 soles. He talks of this criminal trafficking with a laugh, absolutely without reticence and absent any sense of shame.

There are no laws. Each person bears his own penal code in the rifle in his arms and exercises justice as he sees fit, without being called to account. One day in July 1905 when the mixed Peruvian–Brazilian border commission came to the last *puesto cauchero* on the Purus, the commissioners beheld a naked, atrociously mutilated body lying in a clearing amid the *frecheira* trees on the left bank of the river. It was the cadaver of an Amauaca woman. Later it was vaguely explained that she had been killed in an act of vengeance, and nothing more was said about the incident—a highly trivial, virtually meaningless matter in a place frequented by people who pass through but do not settle. They move on, leaving it even sadder with the remains of abandoned *estancias*.

Those *estancias*—from the humble huts of the *peones* to the once lavish dwellings of the *caucheros*—are to be found standing sadly all through the Upper Purus.

One, not far upstream from Shamboyco, especially impressed me when we stopped there.

It had once been a *puesto* of the highest caliber. We got out to look through it. Climbing to the top of the poorly graded incline, we came across the old road, now choked with wild broom bush. We reached the open square where the matted undergrowth was growing through and covering over the heaps of old vessels, repugnant piles of garbage, leftover parts from tools, and mounds of trash left by the inhabitants as they fled. In the center was the main building, half collapsed, roof fallen in, walls akimbo and coming apart, pulling away from studs that themselves were now at a slant. It was held together only by the vines that, having pierced its outer shell, had crawled through its every cranny and wound themselves along its wobbling beams, making them fast, and then reaching back and attaching themselves like cables to the nearest trees, preserved the edifice from complete collapse. The smaller outlying buildings, covered with creepers displaying smiling flowers, were also in a state of collapse, disappearing little by little in the irresistible coils of a forest that was in the process of reconquering its former domain.

We paid little attention, however, to this magnificent reclamation project being carried out by the flora, strewing those deplorable ruins with beautiful garlands and little flowers. The ghost town was not entirely uninhabited.

In one of the better preserved of the outlying buildings, the last inhabitant awaited us. Piro, Amauaca, or Campa, his provenience was indistinguishable. His repulsive appearance transformed the very features of the human species: a huge trunk bloated with malaria dominated, in obvious contrast to thin arms and thin, withered legs, like those of a monstrous fetus.

Crouched in one corner, he contemplated us impassively. He had next to him all his possessions: a bunch of green bananas.

This indefinable thing, who by cruel analogy suggested by the circumstances seemed to us less a man than a ball of *caucho* left behind by the harvesters and simply tossed here by random chance, responded to our questions in a nearly inaudible croak and in a completely incomprehensible language. At the end, with enormous effort he lifted one arm; he slowly extended it out in front of himself as though signaling something far away, beyond all these forests and rivers. And he stammered, letting the arm fall back heavily, as though he had just raised a great weight: "Friends."

We understood: "friends," companions, associates from those busy days of the harvest, who had left for those other places abandoning him here in absolute solitude.

Of the Spanish words he had learned, only that one remained. And this miserable man, murmuring it like a touching gesture of nostalgia, unknowingly demolished with deeply pungent sarcasm the wastrel adventurers who at that very moment were carrying on elsewhere their devastating enterprise: opening up with rifle balls and machete strokes new paths for their frenetic coming and going, and revealing other unknown areas, where they would leave behind, as they had here, in the fallen-in buildings or the pitiful figure of the sacrificed Indian, the only fruits of their tumultuous undertaking, fruits of their role as builders of ruins.

NOTE

1. For example, cases of this sort, related by the Peruvians themselves, are common: A barge leaves Iquitos loaded with the types of merchandise most desired by the river's inhabitants. It stops at a *tambo* on the Ucayali, populated by infidels, or *cholos*. The boss gets out of the boat and invariably has this dialogue with the owner of the site: "Do you have *caucho*?"

"Yes, I do. But it is for buyer F . . . I owe it to him in exchange for the advance he gave me four months ago. His launch should be coming to pick it up a few days from now."

"Don't be a fool, man!" the *cauchero* retorts. And he adds, lying baldly: "F . . . can't come for the *caucho* because his launch is broken down."

"That doesn't matter," the savage demurs. "I intend to keep the bargain by awaiting the instructions he sends me."

The civilized man insists: "And in the meantime you will be hurting yourself, because F . . . will never pay you more than twelve soles per *arroba*, while I will give sixteen *soles* here and now.

The *peón*, eager for the unexpected extra money, wavers; the *cauchero* artfully takes advantage of his vacillation: "Let's go to my launch. I will stand you to a good glass."

They go to the launch. In a short time the drunken *peón* gives the best of his holdings to the *cauchero* for the lowest of prices.

Judas Ahasverus

On Holy Saturday the *seringueiros* of the Upper Purus liberate themselves from their days of sadness. It is the day of alleviation. In their rudimentary conception of life, on this day all evils are sanctified. They believe in a liturgical sanction for even the greatest of transgressions.

On high the Man-God, under the spell of the arrival of his son resurrected and released from human treachery, smiles down complacently on the fierce joy that breaks out here below. And the *seringueiros* raucously avenge themselves upon the sadness of their life.

There are no solemn masses, no magnificent processions; there is no touching foot washing or inspirational preaching. All of Holy Week has represented for them the torturing sameness of that static existence made up of identical days of penury, a permanently bleak environment of sadness and worry that seems like an interminable, anguished Passion Friday stretching forth to the entire year ahead.

Some people recall that during this mournful season in their native lands all activity would be curtailed—streets depopulated, businesses paralyzed, roadways deserted—and that the lights would agonize on flickering candles and voices grow faint in prayer and meditation. A great mysterious silence would fall upon the cities, the villages, and the remote *sertões* where the saddened people identified with God's prodigious sorrow. And they consider, absorbed, that these seven exceptional days, everywhere fleeting and everywhere clearly established as more significant than the other, more numerous days of happiness, are for them here their entire monotonous, obscure, pain-filled, and anonymous existence repeating vexingly an unchanging Via Dolorosa, without beginning or end, in the closed circles of the "paths." Then these simple souls, blocking out the more seductive mirages of the faith, conceive the heavy shadow of a singularly pessimistic outlook on life. Clearly the Universal Redeemer has not redeemed them; he has forgotten them forever, or perhaps has simply not noticed them, relegated as they are to the margins of the solitary river which, in the very rush of its waters, is the first to flee, eternally, from these sad and unfrequented places.

But they do not rebel; they do not blaspheme. The crude *seringueiro*, contrary to the artistic Italian, does not abuse the goodwill of his god by engaging in dramatic outrage. He is stronger than that; he is more worthy. He has resigned himself to his misfortune. He does not grumble. He does not importune. Sometimes anguished prayers rise to heaven bearing a disguised resentment against the deity. But he does not complain. He has a practical, tangible notion, created without deliberation, without the dilution of metaphysics. It is a massive, inexorable, fatalistic notion—a great weight crushing his whole life. And he submits himself to it without the subterfuge of cowardly entreaty set forth on bended knee. That would be a useless effort. His rudimentary outlook is dominated by a perhaps overly objective or ingenuous—but in any case irreducible—conviction, which at every instant his open eyes verify, astonished: he has been excommunicated by the very distance by which he is removed from other men, and the great eyes of God cannot lower themselves to peer into these immense swamps. He sees no value in doing penance, which is just a careful way to rebel, claiming a step up on the indefinite scale of good fortune. There are happier, better protected, more numerous competitors, and—what he sees as most effective—more visible ones: in the chapels, in the churches, in the cathedrals, in the wealthy cities where the pomp of suffering can be readily displayed in a black dress, in the radiance of tears, in making a show of sadness.

Here—his task is to go on, silently, impassively, stoically, in the grand isolation of his misfortune.

Moreover, he is allowed to punish himself only—for the accursed ambition that brought him to this place, thereby to deliver him, hands tied, enslaved, to the deceiving contractors who manipulate him. This sin is its own punishment, transforming his life into an interminable penitence. All he can do is reveal it, tear it out of the shadow of the forests, show it to distant humanity stripped bare in its true, fearsome form.

Now, for that purpose the Church has given him a sinister emissary: Judas. And a single happy day: the Saturday preceding the most sacred of outrages, the most heinous of treasons, the mystical turbulence of the chosen, and the divinization of vengeance.

But the hypertrivialized monster of all places and all times is not up to this complex and weighty mission. He has been too worn down by the passing of the centuries, so trodden down, so diluted, so riven by the stones hurled at him that he has become commonplace in his infinite misery, monopolizing universal hatred, and ever more shrunken before the huge numbers of those who despise him.

It becomes necessary, at a minimum, to accentuate his most distinctive and cruel lines and to depict on his cloth face, in streaks of charcoal, a torture so tragic and in so many ways so close to reality that the eternal condemned man might seem to be resurrected at the same time as his divine victim. It is a practice carried out in a way that defies a more spontaneous repulsion and a more understandable retort, thus fully satisfying the resentful souls of the believers with an image as perfect as possible of his misery and his terrible agony.

And the *seringueiro* throws himself into this prodigious representation aided by his small children, who, in ecstasies of laughter, run noisily about the riverbank in search of loose tufts of straw and discarded pieces of filthy clothing, enchanted with this funambulatory undertaking that so suddenly punctuates the sad monotony of a quiet and unchanging existence.

The Judas is made as he has always been: a pair of pants and an old shirt crudely sewn together and stuffed full of rags and straw. Arms sticking out horizontally, wide apart; legs at an angle, without articulation, without definition, without folds, sticking out alarmingly straight; mounted on a pole in the center of the square. At the top, an inelegant ball representing the head. It is a common mannequin, used everywhere, and it satisfies most people. But it is not sufficient for the *seringueiro*. For him it is merely the block of stone from which the statue is going to be extracted—his masterpiece, the astonishing creation of his crude genius long affected by adversity. Others may distinguish admirable traces of highly subtle irony in it, but for him it is merely the concrete expression of a painful reality.

He begins work up close to the shapeless figure. He accentuates its nose, deepens the orbits of the eyes, reduces the forehead, emphasizes the cheek bones, and sharpens the chin in a slow, careful massage. He paints on eyebrows and patiently opens its eyes with two long curved lines. They are usually sad eyes filled with a mysterious stare. The mouth is drawn in, topped by a sparse moustache that turns down at the ends. It is then dressed with still serviceable cotton pants and shirt, and some old boots with worn-down heels are fastened on.

The *seringueiro* walks back a half dozen paces. He looks it over for some minutes. He studies it.

The children crowding around remain quietly expectant, attending the realization of the concept, which thrills them.

He walks back to his homunculus. He retouches one eyelid and sharpens an expressive curl in the curvature of a lip. He adds a bit more contour to the face, making it more concave. He repositions the head, bends the arms, adjusts and resets the clothing.

A new walk back, measured and slow, looking it over again to capture, in the overall appearance, the exact impression, the synthesis of all those lines. He redoes the task with the patience and the agony of the artist never satisfied with his work. New retouches, more delicate, more painstaking, more careful, more serious: a tenuous softening of a contour, an almost imperceptible trace in the fold of the mouth, an insignificant twist of the neck from which the rag necktie hangs.

Slowly but surely, in an imperceptible transfiguration, the monster changes into a man. At very least the image becomes a fascinating one.

Suddenly the coarse sculptor makes a gesture more moving than Michelangelo's anguished *Parla!* he pulls off his own hat and tosses it on the Judas's head. And all the children shrink back with a cry, seeing portrayed in the disjointed and sinister creation the figure of their own father.

It is dolorous triumph. The *sertanejo* has sculpted the accursed figure in his own image. He has taken revenge on himself. In the final analysis he has punished himself for the accursed ambition that brought him to this land and takes revenge on himself for the moral weakness that shatters his impulse to rebel, pushing it ever further onto the lower plane of this degenerate life where infantile credulity has tied him to this swampy realm controlled by scoundrels who deceive him.

This, however, is not enough to satisfy him. The material image of his unhappiness cannot remain useless in a small clearing along a riverside hut hidden away in the impenetrable denseness that steals away the scene of his perpetually anonymous sorrow from the very eyes of God. The river that passes in front of his door is a roadway to all the earth. Let the whole earth witness his misfortune, his excruciating anguish, his worthlessness, his unjust annihilation shockingly externalized and proclaimed by a strange, mute herald.

Below, built since last evening for this purpose, one sees a raft made of four buoyant poles sturdily held together on cross members. It awaits the macabre traveler. The *seringueiro* conveys it there quickly, dragging it down the slope rutted by the rushing river.

In short order the demonic figure is standing erect, fastened down in the stern of the light craft.

The final adjustments are made: the clothing is straightened one last time, a sack full of gravel and stones is placed on its shoulders, some useless, rusted pistol or worn knife is stuck into its belt. And, giving it a series of curious recommendations or imparting to it the oddest of advice, the *seringueiro* finally pushes the fantastic raft out into the river's current.

Judas made Ahasverus proceed slowly toward the middle of the river. Then the nearest neighbors, who gather curiously along the tops of the banks, begin their raucous participation, saluting the launch with repeated rifle volleys. The balls spatter across the liquid surface, roiling it. They splinter the watercraft. They strike the frightening crewman, passing through it. It teeters on its floating pedestal, pierced by the rifle balls. It vacillates for several minutes as though endeavoring to pick out a route, until finally bringing itself about in the direction of the main flow of the current. And that untoward, tragic, terrifyingly burlesque figure, with its disjointed movements of demon and clown, defying both curses and ridicule, floats away on its doleful voyage without destination and without end, going downstream, ever downstream, twirling about, mocking in every direction as it goes bobbing at the mercy of the currents along the surface of the great water.

Thereafter, it never hesitates. As it moves on, the wandering scarecrow sows desolation and terror in all directions. The birds, stricken with fear, take silent refuge on inner branches. The heavy amphibians protect themselves by diving deep under the surface, frightened of that shadow that, as afternoons wane or morning dawns, lengthens, stretching lugubriously across the river's surface. Men race for their arms and in a fury mixed with fright, making the sign of the cross and cocking their rifles, riddle it piteously.

It does not greet even the poorest hut without taking on a rolling discharge of rifle fire and a stoning.

The rifle balls whistle all around it; they pass through it. The water, scourged by the stones, ripples in expanding circles. The raft lists from side to side, and along with that motion the crewman waves its arms, seemingly acknowledging with clumsy bows the bitter outpouring in which shots, shouts, biting sarcasm, exorcisms, and curses compete. All of this revives again, in the hackneyed word of the backwoodsmen, this echo of a curse that has resonated through twenty centuries: "Be gone, wretch!"

And it *is* gone. It does not stop. It moves farther and farther as it rolls with the water. It frees itself from its persecutors. It glides silently for a long, straight stretch; it rounds the gentle curve of a deserted beach. Suddenly, as it successfully negotiates a bend, another dwelling: women and children surprised at the river's edge, clamoring hastily up the slope, retreating amid outcries and wailing. And immediately thereafter, from the top of the bank, rifle fire, and volleys of stones, and the insults and the taunting.

Two or three minutes of clamor and tumult, until the Wandering Jew frees itself from the range of the rifle fire, going on downstream.

And it keeps on going downstream, downstream . . . after a while it is not floating along in isolation. Companions in misfortune begin to join it on the dolorous road. Other haunting deformities atop similar small rafts delivered over to the whim of the currents, appear from all sides, various in aspect and gesture: some lashed rigidly to the posts holding them up; some tipping about wildly, like drunken men, at the slightest list of the raft; or diviners, arms raised menacingly, hurling curses; others thoroughgoingly humble, bowing in deep abjection; and occasionally, the saddest, those arranged at the end of ropes tied to the top of the slender, arched mast, swinging back and forth . . . hanged.

They pass by in pairs or in lines, going downstream, slowly downstream.

Sometimes the river widens out into an immense circle and gathers in a pool. The current curves and goes in slow circles along the banks, tracing the large spiral of an imperceptible, treacherous whirlpool. The vagabond ghosts float into these enclosures of calm, stagnant water, and for a while they are stranded. They pile up in a group. They mill about. They circle slowly in silent review. Here for the first time the motion-less false stares of their pretend eyes cross. Their paralyzed gestures and rigid bodies move confusedly in ruffled agitation. There is the illusion of a stupendous tumult without sound, of an eerie, highly agitated meet-ing of conspirators in which secrets are shared in the muffled tones of inaudible voices.

Then, one by one, they drift away. They leave, disperse. And moving with the current as it picks up again at the last eddy of the pool, they float on, in rows, one after the other, slowly, processionally, downstream.

"Brazilians"

Peru has two fundamentally distinct histories. One, found in most books, theatrical and noisy, boils down to the melodramatic romance of the instant marshals of the pronunciamentos. The other is obscure and productive. It takes place in the wilderness. It is more moving, more serious, and more complex. It prolongs in other settings the glorious tradition of the wars of independence and—despite its variable elements—has come down to our days so indivisible and seamless that it can be recapitulated in the single term generally adopted for it by the best publicists of that republic: the "eastern question."

The designation is perfect. It denotes a rigorously positive problem in need of solution.

It has not been imposed on the Peruvian through exhaustive argument by sociologists or a statesman's happy inclination, but by material pressures exerted by the environment itself. Restricted to a ribbon of scorched lands between the mountain range and the sea, where for three centuries it has located itself distracted by the pomp of conquistadors and viceroys, the nationality, greatest heir of the equally noteworthy virtues and vices of the knightly and decadent Spain of the seventeenth century, finally came to recognize, through the simple instinct of self-defense, the urgent necessity of abandoning the cloistered isolation that held it apart from all the rest of the earth.

And it began to cross the Andes.

It would take too long to recount its eastward flight in successive inroads along five difficult routes winding maddeningly through the twists and turns of the mountains, climbing along mountainsides thousands of meters high that unite the coastal ports from Mollendo to Paita with the desired areas of "La Montaña," on the far upstream edge of the Amazon that stretches from the "*pongo*," or gorge, of Manseriche to the surging torrents of the affluents of the Urubamba.

Suffice it to note that, after the final eastern range was crossed and the Ucayali basin reached, something in addition to the exuberance of the marvelous valley, capable of regenerating their nationality in decline, became obvious to even the most incurious of pioneers. In a physical anomaly linked to the orthographic contours that predominate in that valley, the fact is that most of their country—generally considered the most Pacific of countries—has its only true sea, capable of linking it through commerce with far-flung points of civilization, in the Atlantic Ocean, to which it is connected by the three long, unimpeded courses of the Purus, the Juruá, and the Ucayali.

No marvel of engineering could offer more than those rivers do. Neither the Oroya Railroad nor the other lines that equal it in the daring of their routes—curving along the sides of nearly vertical mountain walls, winding through tunnels choked with clouds, and running through viaducts high above the abyss—create more practical and more secure transportation systems.

Such exceptional technical requirements are disastrous for industry, making those lines permanently inappropriate for the transport of the products of the east without exorbitant cost—even in the future when the Panama Canal dispenses with the long voyage around Cape Horn.

Thus exit through the Amazon and its southwest tributaries and into the Atlantic became the first clear solution to the problem. And in the new areas set up administratively in the current Department of Loreto there began an intensive development project, which persists and accelerates into our time.

Roads were opened to the rich river valley. Despite a series of setbacks, military and agricultural settlements were continuously planned. In a revival of the apostolic missions, the admirable tradition of the Maynas Jesuits was restarted. A vast regularization of land tenancy was launched. The port of Iquitos was built. To stimulate settlement, all taxes were abolished, allowing man to act freely on that abundant land. At the same time, the geographical expeditions begun by Beltrán and Smith in 1834, in which Castelnau, Maldonado, Raimondi, Tucker, and, in our day, Stiglich have performed so admirably, have headed in every direction, persistent and uninterrupted, on the complex task that rushed to set up a new country.

Calm explorers counterbalance restive *caudillos*. On a coast beset with civil violence and sedition, the chronic incompetence of revolutionary governments became a way of life. The primary motives for the most recent campaign for liberty having been corrupted, the bold vanquishers of power would themselves go too far in a pernicious militarism that was the open sore on an infirm nation. In the flourishing wilderness of "La Montaña," however, with or against the current of unknown rivers; whirling in the dizzying circles of the *muyunas*; piercing straight through in their canoes the lightning currents of the *pongos*; or running abruptly into obstacles in the rapids, geographers, prefects, and missionaries were staking out new territories for a national regeneration. Testing the noblest attributes of their race in an apprenticeship of peril, they went about reconstructing a national character that had been diminished and giving those places, defined in dry, geometric coordinates, a destiny unexpected by History.

In the last analysis the "eastern question" involved, in numerous unknown dimensions, the destiny of all Peru.[1]

The frenzied *caudillos* recognized as much. It was not unusual amid the recklessness and changeability of their actions, between the battles and the executions, for them to stop for a moment and take that persistently desired region into account. Many found themselves transformed and began demonstrating statesmanlike convictions in that regard.

Numerous cases can be cited of such binocular politics, almost exact copies one of the next. Simultaneously destructive and restorative, that politics portrays the physical contrast in the moral order of Peru between the benighted west, in which energies ebb away condemned by the epidemic emotional history of the pronunciamento, and the east, where hope dawns reborn.

Let me cite one example.

In 1841 the republic was on the brink of major catastrophe. Don Agustín Gamarra held power. In his unrestrained actions that Caesarian mestizo reflected the instability of a mixed-blood temperament beset by fears and frustrations deriving from an ascendancy put together by improvisation during the *caudillo* wars.

His government—one set up by the figure who, in his overthrow of the virtuous la Mar, introduced Peru to the regime of the coup d'état— was naturally extremely volatile. This restorer imposed by Chilean arms, by Bulnes, on the ruins of the ephemeral Peru–Bolivia Confederation, beleaguered by frustrated ambitions, by the demands of insatiable mercenaries and the threats of reemerging conspirators, teetered on the edge of that eminence that he had reached by separating himself from his partnership with the *cholos* and cultivating the aristocratic sensibilities of a land that more than any other inherited traditional Spanish haughtiness. At pressing moments his fortune depended on a woman— his wife, a nobly heroic Amazon who on occasion, taking up a sword and spurring on her horse, charged onto the field of battle, even into the hottest point of combat, in order to reanimate the waning dedication of the colonels and the vacillating troops.

Of such a life—both disturbed and hyperemotionalized in so many ways—as was this president's one cannot expect statesmanlike administrative accomplishments. I recount Gamarra's life merely with the artistic interest of one who follows the plot of a fanciful tale marked with dramatic, even awe-inspiring episodes until its end is reached in the glorious and useless sacrifice of the protagonist—in Gamarra's case, before a furious charge by Bolivian lancers on the plains of Viacho.

But, when we turn one of its pages, this surprise jumps out at us:

Citizen Agustín Gamarra, Grand Marshal-Restorer of Peru, distinguished to the nation for valor, eminent, etc.
Considering that for the purpose of promoting steam navigation upon the Amazon River and its tributaries it is necessary to provide facilities and incentives to compensate entrepreneurs.
Decrees: (1) To don Antonio Marcelino Pereira Ribeiro, citizen of Brazil, is granted the exclusive privilege of navigating with steamboats upon the Amazon River, in that part belonging to Peru, and all its tributaries . . .
  (3) The steamboats shall display the Brazilian flag . . .
Given in the Government House in Lima on the 6th of July, 1841.[2]

This decree, the relevant passages of which are excerpted, manifests both the *caudillo*—in the presumptuous self-presentation imparted by the nouns and adjectives made to accompany his name—and also the statesman who first sketched out for his countrymen the regenerating march eastward. But it is not reproduced here merely to point up the contradictory elements in Peruvian history. It also comes to point out the Brazilian figure who would have remained unidentified had he not represented the first in the series of obscure countrymen of ours who have evaded our historical chroniclers but, by dint of their remarkable acts, advance themselves among those who have best served the neighboring country.

Indeed, as the Peruvian march creeps eastward, exposed in all its detail, elaborated in regulations, decrees, circulars, and directives—for it is the supreme political, military, and administrative preoccupation in Peru—one observes in the obligatory and incisive references to the Brazilian dimension the interactive presence of another, counterposed expansion westward, obscure but no less vigorous in its own right. With its effects glimpsed now and again, precisely in the most decisive moments of the Peruvian advance, a whole chapter in our History previously lost or fragmented beyond the limited field of vision of our chroniclers emerges only now, scattered in surprising fragments, between the lines in the History of another people.

Similar demonstrations can be made with other events, ones of which we are equally uninformed. Let me briefly point them out.

The explorations continued during the time when the austere Marshal Castillo governed. Castelnau traveled down from the headwaters of the Urubamba to the banks of the Amazon. In a daring expedition, Maldonado immortalized his name by discovering a new road to the Atlantic following the huge valley of the Madre de Dios. And Raimondi unveiled the Mesopotamian treasures of the 16,000 square leagues of rich land along the courses of the Huallga and the Ucayali. Finally, Montferrir rigorously calculated the bounty of the vast Canaan at 50 million hectares, worth at minimum a half a billion pesos.

The arithmetic became almost lyrical in its relating of such marvelous figures.

The great marshal's government policy benefited immediately from a vigorous patriotic response, as well as from adventurers' desire for fortune.

The Peruvians, long oriented toward the sterile Pacific coast, saw the new world for the first time. And full-blown land conquest was the result.

Then, frustrating the great expectations deriving from so much thoughtful government planning—laws, regulations, and decrees all coming together in a voluminous compendium of fertile and militant administration—there began a disheartening phase of brilliant but abortive initiatives.

Settlements planned and quickly built manifested the phantasmagoria of an artificial progress in those solitary recesses—and soon flickered out completely. By 1854 the governor of Loreto—an obscure pueblo the name of which is distinguished today because it is applied to an entire region—in reporting on the status of two settlements that had been estab lished there, centralized in Caballo-Cocha near the Brazilian border, referred to them as completely extinct. Similar setbacks were general across the region.

Those results were natural ones. Waves of humanity coming into virgin territory do not simply stop. What characterizes them in their first stages is an inevitable instability imposed by the energies inherent in the movement itself. Preceding cultural equilibrium comes the search for immediate fruits or riches, as though providing the new arrivals, in the wandering life of gathering, extraction, herding, or hunting, with the necessary reconnaissance of their new habitat before they choose a more settled lifestyle.

What is involved is the eternal social function of nomadism, which even in Peru manifested itself in the devastating activity of the quinine harvesters called *cascarilleros*, who opened up the previously unknown lands that run from the Carabaya hills to the remote headwaters of the Beni.

By then, however, that particular incentive had become extinct.

By that time a tenacious explorer, Marckam, commissioned by the British government, was active in the regions of *calisaya* quinine. He was so successful in transplanting to India that element of Peruvian fortune that by 1862 more than 4 million trees, with the incredible production of 370 tons, launched from Darjeeling a competition that triumphed on the first assault. Thus the lands so fervently desired showed themselves to their new settlers despoiled of the kinds of resources that regularly arise to keep the grandiose hopes of immigrants from being dashed.

Certainly the fibers for the hats created by the gracious industry of the Mayobamba women would not satisfy them; nor would the gold-bearing gravel of the slopes of the Pastaza, guarded by the ferocious Huambizas.

Thus all the acts, magnificent decrees, lucid regulations, and generous concessions of land issued by the second Castilla government would
have ended up in the most lamentable of failures if, precisely in the last
period of his presidency, and in the same year—1862—in which Indian
cultivation of quinine was depriving the wilderness of its greatest allure,
an anonymous man, one more humble immortal who has escaped our
historiography, had not appeared and immediately eclipsed the weight-
iest administrative initiatives, offering Peruvians the animating antidote
that would sustain them to this day in their turn to the Amazon.

A Brazilian discovered *caucho*, or, at least, established the industry
of its extraction. I do not go alone in my reconstruction of this chapter
in our History, which, if fully developed later by a historian, might be
entitled: "Brazilian Expansion in the Amazon."

A trustworthy narrator tells us:

> Before the year 1862 the incalculable wealth in elastic gum had not yet been
> explored . . . After some Brazilians entered the Department, principally the
> industrious José Joaquim Ribeiro, this product began to figure on the ledger
> of those that the Department exports to Brazil. The quantity first exported
> was 2,088 kilograms, result of test harvesting carried out by that Brazilian,
> who would have contributed greatly to the development of that industry
> if, when he was launching it, he had not encountered problems born
> of the greed of some subordinate agents who practiced every sort of
> stratagem against him.[3]

I shall not remark on the Peruvian authorities' antagonism. It was an
attitude of long standing. As early as 1811 don Manuel Ijurra fumed that
"the Brazilians closest to Peru have the barbarous custom of mounting
military expeditions with the object of attacking the Maynas Indians,
often in direct disregard of the authorities." And he represented the
Brazilians as "absolute monopolists of the import-export business."[4] Five
years later, in an alarming directive, the subprefect of Maynas requested
urgent preparations "against the possibility that the Brazilians residing
in Caballo-Cocha might withdraw from that province, if not peaceably
then by force." And he painted them as practicing the most horrible of
abuses. Finally the governor-general of Misiones (1849) declared that all
Brazilians entering that department would be required to carry passports,
stammering in a stiff Spanish the following extremely odd reasoning:
"No value whatsoever is being derived from the presence of these

Brazilian traders; nor are there bayonets enough to contain them. They do whatever they want, plying the rivers, extracting berries, butter, salt, and other foodstuffs."5

Let us proceed no farther.

What is easily deduced from such lines, which could be multiplied, is that a formidable invasion was reaching westward in defiance of a hatred of foreigners—an invasion that spread along the valley of the great river, through Loreto, Caballo-Cocha, Moremote, Perenate, Iquitos, all the way to Nauta at the mouth of the Ucayali and up the Ucayali to beyond Pachitea. That invasion has left the indelible traces of its passing at the most varied of points, in numerous places along the winding wilderness trails, and even in the customs that have come to exist in those places.

If one were to write its history he could counterpose the official diatribes of the terrified subprefects, whose language became stronger and stronger as that mute conquest of the land progressed, to the concepts of such as Antonio Raimondi. But the remarkable Joaquim Ribeiro, whom the great Peruvian naturalist found on the banks of the Itaya in possession of the best lands in the department, concretizes the undeniable response. Such trifling hindrances did not bother him. After 1871, with the industry of extraction created, rubber became the principal export product of Loreto. And the bands of the extractors, with no official incentives, arriving spontaneously from everywhere and operating in the most unfrequented parts of the forest, put a quick end to the almost century-old initiative so often riven with setbacks.

The entire east was opened up.

But there is one negative to that picture.

The exploitation of *caucho* as the Peruvians practice it, with its felling of the trees and the constant movement in search of undiscovered stands of *Castilloa* in an endless professional nomadism, leads them to practice all manner of abuse in the inevitable confrontations with the natives, and thus brings with it the systematic disruption of society. The *cauchero*, eternal seeker of new locations, has no relationship to the land. In his primitive activity, he develops prioritarily the attributes of cleverness, agility, and strength. It involves, in sum, a barbarous individualism. There is a lamentable involution in a man perpetually away from society, wandering from river to river, from thicket to thicket, ever in search of virgin forest in which to hide or take refuge, like a fugitive from civilization.

His passage there has been devastating. After thirty years of population, the banks of the Ucayali, in the past so graced by the abnegation of the Sarayaco missionaries, today manifest an indescribable moral decay in their dingy little settlements.

Colonel Pedro Portillo, present-day prefect of Loreto, who visited there in 1899, indignantly denounced them for that: "there is no law there . . . The strongest, the one with the most rifles, owns the justice." He also condemned the scandalous trafficking in slaves.[6] And, in the same vein, many others who have passed though, a list of whom would be too long to reproduce, testify in detailed narratives to the regime of lawlessness that became the norm in those lands—and continues to grow, following the tracks of men who pass through the wilderness whose only goal is to barbarize the barbarians.

Now, in clear anticipation of the problems attendant upon that exploitation, which at the same time was the vehicle for the full development of its dominion in the east, the Peruvian government never renounced its initial intent to engage in large-scale settlement. And in order simultaneously to guarantee use of the best route to the Amazon, which runs through the Ucayali—from the terminus station at Oroya to the principal tributaries of the Pachitea—in 1857 it established on the Pozuzo River, one of those tributaries, the German settlement that more than any other monopolized its uninterrupted attention and concern.

The situation was indeed remarkable. Located on incredibly fertile lands halfway to Iquitos, near the navigable tributaries of the Ucayali, the nucleus that was established was, militarily and administratively speaking, the strongest strategic point in the struggle with the wilderness. Hence the justification for all the efforts and the extraordinary expense to encourage the rapid development that those excellent conditions naturally favored.

But the plan did not meet expectations. Much as happened in Loreto, the new settlers, albeit more tenacious, ended up in an unpredictable decline. The colony became paralyzed, stunted, there among the splendors of the forest. It was reduced to rudimentary productive practices that barely met its own consumption. And the all but negligible demographic progress could produce nothing more than a lymphatic generation in which the hardy Prussian stock degenerated to the level of the withered capacities of the Quichua. When he visited there in 1870, Colonel Vizcarra, prefect of Huanuco, was shocked and moved: the settlers presented themselves to him in tatters and starving, asking for bread and for clothing with which to cover themselves. The romantic don Manuel Pinzás, who described the trip, paints for us in long, lachrymose sentences the content of that "heart-rending scene," suspending it between two rigid exclamation points.[7]

Moreover, some five years later Dr. Santiago Tavara saw it in the same tones when he described Admiral Tucker's first trip.

Finally, thirty years later, on his passage from the Ucayali, Colonel Portillo received accurate information about the nucleus of that settlement: it had become a terrifying wasteland. There the first settlers and their degenerate offspring, victims of an irremediable fanaticism, were to be found indulging in the lethargic practices of doing penance, praying, telling rosaries over and over, and chanting interminable litanies in a scandalous parallel with the monkeys of the forest.[8]

To further aggravate the disappointment at that complete failure of the favored colony, that passer-through, who is one of the most lucid Peruvian politicians of our time, only days before had passed through Puerto Victoria at the confluence of the Pichis and the Palcazu where the Pachitea is formed. There he witnessed a completely different phenomenon. In fact, Puerto Victoria had come into being and developed, turning into the most active and prosperous *estancia* in the area, without the Peruvian government even knowing of its original existence.

It had never planned to colonize in that area

The place had been considered ill-favored. It was surrounded by what were among the wildest of the South American savages: the Campas of Pajonal to the south and to the north the indomitable Caxibos, who, in 1866 at Conta-Isla, downstream from Puerto Victoria, had beheaded the naval officers Tavara and West. Prefect Benito Araña, who had visited there that same year, mounted a full military operation with two steamboats and an artillery launch, to avenge the bloody affront. He went ashore, invaded the forest, engaged in small skirmishes with lots of gunfire, and returned in a highly unusual triumph—one with the savages hot on his heels shooting arrows after him. He embarked amid the tumult of his people victorious—and fleeing. They bombarded the riverbanks furiously and returned downstream in flight, leaving a novelistic token of their violent and embarrassing undertaking in the toponym "Playa del Castigo" ("Retribution Beach").

For the next three decades that sinister region remained in the isolation in which the terrified people wished to leave it.

Until, entering from the west and overcoming the strong currents of the Pachitea with the strength of powerful paddlers in narrow dugouts, a group of undaunted adventurers traversed it from one end to the other, reaching all the way to the confluence of the Pichis.

They were broad-shouldered *caboclos* with dull, dark skin and dry, powerful musculature. They were not *caucheros*. With them speech did not resonate with noisy braggadocio. Instead of a *tambo* they improvised the lean-to *tejúpar*. They did not carry the *cuchillo*, a cross between a dagger and a short knife. Instead they bore in their belts bush knives as long as swords.

They prepared themselves without fanfare for the undertaking, and they slowly penetrated the forest.

The specific events involved with that daring entry, doubtless highly dramatic, are unknown. The Caxibos have their ferocity inscribed in their very name. "Caxi," "bat"; "bo," "similar to." Figuratively, bloodsuckers. Even in their rare moments of joviality those barbarians are frightening; their laughter reveals teeth stained with the black juice of the chonta palm. Or they stretch out face down, mouths close to the ground, howling the long notes of a savage chant.

They have borne three hundred years of catechism untouched in their savagery. They are still the wildest of the tribes in the Ucayali Valley.

As far as anyone can tell, their presence did not discourage the new pioneers.

For the bloody savage now had before him, taking his measure, a more fearsome adversary than he: the *jagunço*.

These recent arrivals were Brazilians from the *sertão*. Their leader: Pedro C. de Oliveira, yet another of the obscure fighters who sporadically appear in the productive moments that dot the events of a highly unusual history. Despite his nationality, in January 1900 he was named governor of the entire area of which his *barracão* was the center.[9]

Colonel Portillo was the recipient there of simple hospitality without the ceremonial pomp of lavish gifts so characteristic of our obscure *gens*. Every observation contained in his report—from the first day to his taking leave of the "very estimable family of Mr. Oliveira"— bespeaks the pleasure that he derived from seeing the vibrant *estancia*, at the center of rich productivity, intelligently situated with the numerous dwellings circled at the top of the bank on the left side of the river. The *estancia* was reached by climbing a long, sturdy stairway. What especially captivated him were the calm, vigorous men who manifested in an unpretentious way their triumph over the savage and the land. Finally, it did not escape his watchful notice that without decrees or subventions that foreigner had solved the problem that had bedeviled the government of his country by founding in the most strategic location the *estancia* that controlled the "central road" to Amazonia. He said so quite openly: "Puerto Victoria was the most advantageous location for the military garrison and customs house to protect imports and exports from the colony of Chanchamayo, the north of Pajonal, Tarma, and the 'Montañas' of Palcazu, Matro, and Pozuzo."

Colonel Portillo concluded, "The Oliveira house should be taken by the Supreme Government as the most appropriate location for the administrative headquarters, the customs house, and the military post."

The recommendation was accepted. A decree from President Pierola ordered the demarcation of Puerto Victoria in order to establish a police precinct that would protect the settlers of those lands. In an expression of jealousy at the advantageous situation that Oliveira had acquired, he revealed his intention to establish exclusive possession: "not permitting any settler whatsoever within the radius of one kilometer."[10]

Peru had a first-class river *estancia*. And the Brazilians withdrew.

Five years passed.

In 1905 the Parisian tourist J. Delbecque came down the Pachitea en route to the Amazon and would not have noticed the formerly flourishing *estancia* if he had not been accompanied by some tame Indians who knew the area.[11]

At the top of the bank, which the waters were in the process of undermining, one could see only a few fallen roofs and the remnants of productive fields, now choked by wild holm.

The port was a ruin.

Like everyone who goes through that area on the journey from Iquitos, the traveler stayed there for several hours in order to dry wet clothing—in the heat of a fire made with the fallen doors and collapsed jambs of the former dwellings. He meditated, melancholically, that if matters continued that way Puerto Victoria would soon be only a memory.

Then he went on downstream rowing at full speed, fleeing that region that had been depopulated to the point of complete abandonment.

NOTES

1. "It is evident that, at the bottom of this issue there lies a pressing necessity for the republic . . . the destinies of Peru cannot be fulfilled until that area is under our control." Dr. Y. Capelo, *Exposición histórica de la vía central* (1898).

2. *El peruano,* vol. 8, no. 9.

3. J. Wilkens de Matos, *Dicionário topográfico do Departamento de Loreto* (Pará, 1874), 30–31.

4. Manuel Ijurra, *Resumen de los viajes a las montañas de Maynas* (1811–1815).

5. *Colección de leyes, decretos, etc., referentes al Departamento de Loreto,* tomo 5, p. 198; tomo 7, 5.

6. *Colección de leyes, decretos, etc., referentes al Departamento de Loreto,* tomo 3, p. 506.

7. M. J. Pinzás, *Diario de la exploración de los ríos Palcazu, Matro y Pachitea* (Huanuco, 1870).

8. *Colección de leyes, decretos, etc., referentes al Departamento de Loreto,* tomo 3, p. 531.

9. *Registro oficial del Departamento de Loreto* (1900), 10.

10. *La montaña* (1899), 26.

11. J. Delebecque, *À Travers l'Amérique de Sud* (1907).

Transacreana

In the way that it presents the area west of the Madeira, the map of Amazonia is a diagram of its initial settlement. The history of the new region, rather than being written, must be drawn. It isn't read, it is seen. It can be summarized in the long, curving arcs of the Purus, the Juruá, and the Javari.

These are natural lines of communication and transportation that no others can rival in supporting a far-flung dominion. Geometrically, the beds of those river valleys, running at an angle to the meridians and almost parallel to each other—generally southwest to northeast—enable movement forward in latitude and longitude at the same time. Physically, apart from artificial obstacles created by their current state of abandonment, they stretch out unimpeded. Their most important dimensions are, however, blocked. In most Amazonian rivers, and especially in the Ucayali Valley, accumulating impediments have given rise to strange geographical terms. One cannot cite just one of them. Not dizzying *pongos* nor steep rapids nor swirling whirlpools, nor even maddening "devil's turns."

Hence this highly indicative historical consequence: while on the Tocantins, the Tapajós, the Madeira, and the Rio Negro, settlement begun in colonial times has struggled or has even become retrograde—a fact profiled in the ruins of the small settlements, fallen in with undermined banks—here it has progressed in an unforeseeable a manner, conforming to the topography of the river banks. In fewer than fifty years it has led to the expansion of national borders.

It was inevitable. Upon entering the Purus or the Juruá, the foreigner would not see himself as lacking resources for an exceptional commercial venture. A practical canoe and pole or paddle would outfit him for the most amazing voyage. The river would bear him along, guide him, provide nourishment, and protect him. He needed only to gather the precious products from the forest banks, fill his primitive boats with them, and return back downstream, sleeping on top of a fortune acquired with no work. Thanks to its millennarian warehousing of riches, the profligate land has made cultivation unnecessary. It has opened itself up to man with marvelous watery roadways. It has imposed on him only the task of harvesting. In short, nomadism is a logical course for him to take.

The name *montaria*, "mount," given to his light, swift dugout, is apt. It has related him to these level solitudes much as the horse adjusts the Tartar to the steppes. This single difference: while the Kalmuck has, in the infinity of points on the horizon, an infinity of routes to attract him to a nomadism that can spread out in any direction from his yurt—which, even after it is moved to a new location seems motionless on the unending circle of the plains—the Amazonian water pilot, subject to linear routes, held to immutable directions, remains for a long period of time trapped between the banks of rivers. He can detour barely a few leagues, on the tributaries' lateral courses. In contrast to common belief, those complexly interwoven networks do not mix the waters of the different rivers by means of anastomoses winding across the marshy plains. The side channel always returns to the principal bed from which it split off. The *igarapé* ends up in the lake it fed at high water so that it could be fed by it in turn at low water, running in opposite directions according to the season of the year; or it empties out on swampy flatlands hidden by the amphibian florula of the vine-choked *igapós*. Between one watercourse and the other a strip of forest stands in place of the nonexistent mountain. It is the divider. It separates. It divides the masses of settlers who have come to the area into long, isolated roadways.

Along with the highly favorable natural conditions, then, the following downside has been observed: man, instead of mastering the land, becomes enslaved to the river. The population has not expanded; it has stretched. It has progressed in long lines or turned back on itself, all without leaving the waterways along which it is channeled—tending to become immobile while appearing to progress. Progress, despite the many advances and retreats, is in fact illusory. The adventurers who set out, penetrate deep into the land, and exploit it merely return along the same routes, or follow again, monotonously, the same invariable itineraries. In the end, the short but highly restless history of these new regions, a few variants aside, has imprinted itself totally, concretely, according to those long lines opening to the southwest: three or four channels, three or four river profiles, snaking endlessly through a wilderness.

Now this discouraging social dimension, created principally by river conditions otherwise so favorable, can be corrected by the transverse linking of the great valleys.

The idea is neither original nor new. With admirable foresight the rough settlers of those distant areas put it into practice long ago with the creation of the first portages.

The portage—legacy of the heroic activity of the *bandeirantes* shared today by the Amazonian, the Bolivian, and the Peruvian—is a cross path that runs from the terrain of one river course to that of another.

Originally twisting and short, running out in the density of the forests, the portage reflects the indecisive march of the society that, nascent and tottering, first abandoned the river's lap to walk on its own. And it has grown along with that society. Today those narrow courses a meter wide, cleared by bush knife, running in all directions, intertwining in innumerable turns and crossings, linking the separate tributaries of all the headwaters, from the Acre to the Purus, from the Purus to the Juruá, from it to the Ucayali, trace the contemporary history of the new territory in a way totally opposite to earlier subservience to the determining power of the great natural arteries of communication.

In their twists and turns, determined by the highest lines of the low banks, one feels a strange, anxious movement—a movement of revolt. In treading them, man is a rebel. He aggresses against the generous and treacherous nature that has enriched and has killed him. Those old supports that are the rivers so repel him that in this greatest of Mesopotamias he practices the anomaly of navigating on dry land. Or, rather, the following transfiguration of that act: he transports from one river to another the boat that previously transported him. In fine, in an increasing affirmation of will, he extends from one river to the next, reconceived with the aid of the infinite links of the *igarapés*, the imprisoning network of ever smaller and more numerous connections that will shortly deliver over to him a mastered land.

And from the Acre to the Yaco to the Tauamano to the Orton, from the Purus to the Madre de Dios to the Ucayali to the Javari, treading freely all corners of the territory, the Acreans, liberated from the old mark of unification with the distant Amazon that had kept them dispersed and subordinate to the remote coast, as they travel each of those daring roads are securing a tangible symbol of independence and possession.

Let us take one example of witness, by a foreigner.

In 1904 the Peruvian naval officer Germano Stiglich encountered various Brazilians on the Javari. They astonished him with the simple narrative of a routine crossing, in the light of which his most far-flung travels as an eminent explorer were greatly diminished. He registered it in one of his reports: those frontiersmen entered at the Javari and went up the Itacoaí to its headlands. They went from there across country searching for the headwaters of the Ipixuna, found them, crossed them, and came down that small tributary to reach the Juruá. They then traveled on it to São Felipe, where they turned and went onto the Tarauacá, the Envira, and the Jurupari, as far as their light canoes could go. They left them there and again set out across country to reach the Purus in the environs of Sobral. They came down the great river for 760 kilometers in a boat to the mouth of the Ituxi. Following that river, after another cross-country portage, they reached the Abunã, which they came down, finally reaching the left bank of the Madeira.

That route, if one adds 20 percent to the straight measurement to account for actual distance traveled, is calculable at a length of three thousand kilometers, or twice the traditional path of the *bandeirantes* between São Paulo and Cuiabá. Those obscure pioneers had prolonged into our day the heroic tradition of incursions—the only aspect of our History that is unique.

That itinerary, however, is very long, turning as it does in overly wide arcs. Let us cut it down on the basis of some accurate data.

Setting out from Remate dos Males, near Tabatinga on the Javari, the traveler can at any time of year ply the Ituí in one day, covering 140 kilometers. He can then proceed southeast by land on solid roads over the 190-kilometer portage that cuts across the various headwaters of the Jutaí and ends in São Felipe on the banks of the Juruá. It is only five days' march. He can go in a boat up the Tarauacá to the mouth of the Envira and from there to the mouth of the Jurupari, seeking its headwaters. It is a trek that would cover at maximum 350 kilometers, which he could accomplish in little more than a week. He makes his way along the short portage that would bring him to the Furo do Juruá and, going down it for two days, he would reach the Purus. From there to the mouth of the Yaco it is 392 kilometers, which could be run in two days by launch, if the needed minimal upkeep of the river were performed. The headquarters of the prefecture of the Upper Purus, twenty-four kilometers away, can be reached in two hours by river. From there, over the Oriente portage, with a length of twenty-five leagues, normally covered in five days, one can reach the rubber tract of Bajé on the left bank of the Acre. Crossing that river and continuing east across the last tributaries of the Iquiri and the Campos do Gavião, the traveler can go to the Abunã, downstream from the mouth of the Tipamanu and thence to the Beni, at the confluence of the Madeira, covering close to 300 kilometers by land in eight days.

In this fashion, in little more than a month of travel, covering 907 kilometers by water and 660 by land, he can go diagonally from Tabatinga to Villa Bella, from one end of Amazonia to another, in an itinerary of 250 leagues.

Those numbers lack the rigor of real measurement, but the variance cannot be more than perhaps one-tenth, except in the case of the fallible data relating to navigation of the Tarauacá and the overland trek from the Jurupari to the Purus.

Let us exclude them, then, in this variant: departing from the same point on the banks of the Javari and plying the Itacoaí to its highest headwaters, the traveler can use the old portage of the Ipixuna, which will take him to the Juruá and to Cruzeiro do Sul, capital of the Department, in a march that is not much longer than the prior one through São Felipe.

Going from Cruzeiro do Sul to the headquarters of the Departments of the Purus and of Acre eliminates the problems in the former route involved with the precarious and exhausting river trip.

The long rectilinear segment of 605 kilometers that follows the Cunha Gomes line is precisely the planned route of a notable portage that would link together the three administrative seats. Allowing a generous 20 percent on that distance, one calculates a length of 726 kilometers, or exactly 110 leagues, which can be covered by horse in fewer than twelve days.

It should be observed in passing that this project is not one drawn up according to the arbitrary lines to which "map explorers" are accustomed—according to the "well-known gesture that had Czar Nicholas I scratching out a road from St. Petersburg to Moscow with his thumbnail."

It rests instead on practical knowledge—absent azimuths or aneroid readings, but concrete nonetheless and therefore definitive. The first segment, perpendicular to the valley of the Tarauacá, planned by General Taumaturgo de Azevedo, is now in great part open due to the activity of a *seringueiro* from Cocamera. It stretches over terrain so favorable to land travel that, once the road is complete, as the former prefect declares in his penultimate report, "one will travel from the Juruá to the Tarauacá on horseback in four days." To make such a trip currently "in a steamboat that makes few stops and turns at the mouth of the Tarauacá would take at least fifteen days."

The intermediate segment, from Barcelona or Novo Destino to the confluence of the Caeté into the Yaco, studied by the prefecture of the Upper Purus, would be easy to execute over a small, flood-free high plain. And the last, from the Yaco to the Acre, has long had regular traffic.

In this manner the great 726-kilometer roadway linking the three departments and easily extendable on one side all the way to the Amazon by means of the Javari and on the other side all the way to the Madeira by means of the Abunã has been completely reconnoitered and in great part is already in use.

The intervention of the federal government is urgently needed to perform the basic task of linking together the several discrete initiatives and giving incentive to the project.

The project should, however, consist in the establishment of a railroad—the only such road both urgent and indispensable in the entire Acre territory.

Let us anticipate an initial objection.

The physical geography of the Amazon is always cited as an obstacle to this kind of project. But those who adduce it, in arguments that I do not consider it necessary to reproduce here, must be ignorant of

Indian railways. In fact, in Hindustan proper the surface features, the alluvial soil made up of sand and clay laid down in indiscriminate deposits, and the climatic conditions are almost identical to ours. There, as in Amazonia, the rivers are characterized by their large size, excessive volume at high water, amount of flooding, and changeable channels in ever wandering riverbeds. The hydrography of the innumerable *nullahs* winding through the terrain repeats the chaotic hydrography of our *igarapés*. Indeed, the Purus, the Juruá, the Acre, and their tributaries do not vary as much in their courses and regimen as do the Ganges and the rivers of the Punjab, the bridges over which represented the greatest challenge that British engineering had to overcome.

In India, just as in our case, there was no shortage of professionals who were intimidated by the problems presented by the natural conditions—forgetting that engineering exists precisely to overcome such problems. When the "Kennedy memorandum," which was the germ of the Hindu transportation system, was discussed, Colonel Grant of the Bombay Corps of Engineers engaged in a wry bit of humor by proposing that for the entire length of the line the tracks be suspended eight feet above the ground by means of regular series of chains on rigid facing posts. He thus challenged the magnificent humor of his phlegmatic colleagues. The hardy railroadmen met that challenge in overwhelming fashion: with the West Indian Peninsular Railroad. And in so doing they raised railroad engineering to new heights, fulfilling one of its civilizing formulas, first enunciated by Mac-George: "In every country it is necessary that railway should be laid out with reference to the distribution of the population and to the necessities of the people, rather than to the mere physical characteristics of its geography."

Now in our case even the physical and geographical characteristics are favorable.

Unlike the rail beds in the south of our country, the road from Cruzeiro do Sul to the Acre will not go parallel to the general direction of the great valleys because it has a different function. In the south, particularly in São Paulo, the rail lines describe the classical lines of penetration, moving the people toward the heart of the country. In this corner of Amazonia, as we have seen, that function is performed by the watercourses. The projected rail line will have the function of moving from one place to another the people who already live here. Its function is that of auxiliary to the rivers. Therefore it should cut across the valleys.

Hence this necessary consequence: it has to follow the low terrain that divides the lateral tributaries and in so doing will avoid the obstacles presented by the confused hydrography.

By contrast, south of the eighth parallel, the *facies* of the enormous Amazonian *várzea* still predominates but in attenuated form. The tumultuous inconstancy of the waters does not deploy itself in as many curves or as changeably. The terrain, stretching out in gentle rolling hills with an average height of two hundred meters, is generally solid and stands above the high water level. I have walked it at various points. It is visibly clear that one is standing on older, more defined, and more stable formations than those of the immense post-Quaternian plain on which one can still sense the last geological transformation of the Amazon, in its inevitable conflict between the inconstant watercourses and the unstable *várzea*.

Beyond this, the natural obstacles will be either reduced or nearly eliminated by choosing routes that take them well into account. The initial installation of the rail line in question should be carried out on the basis of the least costly technical specifications: a single, reduced-gauge line—0.76 meters, 0.91 meters, or, in the maximum, one meter between rails. That will allow for the steepest grades and the sharpest curves, giving the line the flexibility to make turns in order to seek the highest and most stable ground, which will keep the grade above high water marks along routes approximately at land level. It should start off as have the greatest current railways: at maximum, rails at eighteen kilos per running meter, able to handle lightweight locomotives of fifteen to twenty total tons adhesion weight; curves with down to a fifty-meter radius; and grades of up to 5 percent according to the character of the land.

There is no railway better in this regard than the Central Pacific in Nevada, with its narrow gauge and absence of ballast, twisting, with similar light rails, over ninety-meter curves and winding along slopes with unclassifiable ramps. Or the Trans-Siberian Railroad, where thirty-ton locomotives pulling 1/6 adhesion weight over nineteen-kilo rails and traveling with a speed of twenty kilometers per hour not infrequently are forced to go in reverse when they meet harsh headwinds off the steppes.

To be sure, such a superstructure, to which one must add the imperfectness of the rolling stock, both traction and transport, will support only a significantly reduced traffic capacity. But, much like the Union Pacific, the Acrean Line is not designed to meet the demands of some nonexistent clientele but to create the one that should exist.

Like the American lines, it should be built quickly in order then to be rebuilt slowly.

Such a process is in fact the norm.[1] All the great rail lines, in their beginnings have avoided the most formidable obstacles they faced by using the most basic resources at their disposal to cross the lowest places and avoid the biggest cuts. That process has enabled them to continue laying track, first put down like wild, imperfect roads of battle against the wilderness. And as though to justify that assertion, we can remind ourselves that the first engineer of the same rudimentary structures of wood palings and bridges—which are being built today just as they were two thousand years ago, rough-hewn and erected in lines on the *styli fixi* of round posts—was Caesar.

The roads then evolve and grow, improving the various parts of their complex structure, as though they were enormous living organisms being transfigured by the very life and progress they awaken.

That is what will happen with the line I project here. Its social implications are evident from the first words of this article. Those implications have not been set out in detail because many of them are intuitive and involve multiple effects, which run from the simple concrete fact of population redistribution—siting with greater certainty the nuclei of settlements or agricultural areas and delimiting legally the unassigned lands—to quicker, less cumbersome, and firmer administration of public authority, which currently is triply divided, spread across the three administrative seats that are required purely because of the vicissitudes of geography.

Such results would in and of themselves justify exceptional expenditures.

The following, however, are more open to conjecture. After immediate action by the government and definitive planning, everything leads one to believe that the three principal sections that the railway would include—the segments from the Juruá to the Purus, from the Purus to the Yaco, and from there to the Acre—engaged simultaneously by our military engineers and favored by the easy transport of the necessary materials along those rivers themselves, can be constructed in an expeditious manner and with the resources of local income.

Its engineering works will be insignificant, the most serious being the construction of small bridges and earthworks as well as the extensive clearing, forty meters wide, to achieve maximum clearance for the roadbed.[2]

Not only will the line not need extensive developments to climb high ground but it will also not need tunnels to go through such ground, or major cuts, or viaducts, or even the three great bridges—over the Tarauacá, the Purus, and the Yaco—that might at first seem absolutely indispensable. The station at the terminus of each of the three aforementioned segments can serve as well as the station for navigation of its corresponding river, and, in the first stage of development, the transfers from one bank to the other will be able to be made without significant disturbance of what will naturally be relatively sparse traffic.

Thus costly services will be able to be put off, to be effected gradually in the future according to circumstances. The road will grow with the population. And even though it may stretch out over the enormous distance of 726 kilometers and be limited to one track plus the necessary sidings, allowing the minimal velocity of twenty kilometers per hour, it will be negotiable end to end in a mere thirty-six hours—which would increase to forty-eight when the hours necessary to cross the rivers are added in.

The trip from Cruzeiro do Sul to the Acre will thus be doable in two days. Currently that trip, in the most propitious seasons of the year, takes more than a month.

The conclusion is inalterable. Let us not waste time enumerating the enormous effects.

Let us instead examine another dimension of the question.

Americans have defined railroad engineering in this concise and irreducible formula: "the art of making a dollar earn the highest possible interest."

Let us bow to that barbarously utilitarian precept.

The economic value of the proposed project is incalculable. That fact can be evidenced in multiple forms, those most worthy of credit being—naturally—the furthest in the future: ones deriving from the inevitable progress of the impacted regions.

It would take too long to list each and every effect. Let us indicate one only—and one that is proximate, immediate, and thus recommends itself to even the most resistant outlooks.

For the next-to-last business year of 1905, according to the most reliable documents, the harvest of rubber in the three affected departments, between the Cunha Gomes line and the neutral strip, was as follows:

Juruá River	3,382,134 kilograms
Acre and Purus	5,256,984 kilograms
TOTAL	8,639,118 kilograms

With the current prices varying between the extremes of 3,865 reis and 6,346, one can estimate, in round numbers, an average of 5,000 per kilo and, as a result, the total value of the production at 43,195,590,000 reis, resulting in export tax revenues (23 percent) of 9,934,985,700.

The figures are clear and undeniable.

Now these yields will tend to double, not by dint of some development in the distant future but rather through the simple fact of opening up the rail line.

The demonstration is straightforwardly graphic and readily visualized.

The tapping of the rubber trees, as everyone knows, generally operates in the long strips of the forest mass that flank the two banks of the rivers. The "centers" adjacent to the most highly developed *barracões* are few and ordinarily not very distant. Strictly speaking, these are not surface areas being harvested from but only strips. And with the aid of the existing data, they can be measured with reasonable accuracy. Along the Purus, they stretch from Barcelona to Sobral; on the Yaco, from Caeté to a little beyond the *seringal* of São João; from Cruzeiro do Sul to the mouth of the Breu on the Juruá; and on the Acre, from Porto Acre to not far above the confluence of the Xapuri. If we add to those large strips the smaller ones on the Tarauacá, the Envira, and the Jurupari, we get approximate total dimensions of 150 leagues of strips being harvested, presuming that all are currently in operation—which is not always the case. That extension is, then, a maximum; it is the graphic, visible definition of the current economic import of the territory.

It derives, as one can see, merely from the courses of the rivers.

The new rail line will, naturally, itself represent a "path" providing entry of new workers for the quick harvest of products that up to today have not required any effort at cultivation. Rather than a railroad it will in fact be an enormous, 120-league "path," almost the total size of the stretches currently being harvested. Now, in contrast to the elastic *Castilloas* that produce *caucho*, the *Heveae brasilienses* are characterized by a rather even distribution throughout the forests. Thus, reliably calculated, the proportion necessary to quickly reimburse the immediate cost of the planned rail line, which will inevitably be built in a more or less proximate future according to the route I have traced out, cannot be considered conjectural.

One must add to its value in and of itself those values deriving from its route and that route's articulation with other lines of transport.

The Madeira-Mamoré rail line, once completed, will attract it eastward, irresistibly, through the commonplace phenomenon of the attraction of systems. It will, then, cross the Acre and go in search of the Madeira at the confluence of the Abunã, or at Villa Bella, suddenly doing away with all the inconvenience associated with three long, roundabout river voyages. At the same time, at its other end, spreading out westward, going up the Moa and passing over the low hills of Contamana, it will reach the Ucayali, transferring to the Madeira port town of Santo Antônio part of the commercial gravitation of Iquitos. At that point the very modest "Transacrean Line," almost local in character, designed to deal with peculiar hydrographic conditions, will have been transformed into an international roadway with an extraordinary destiny.

Let us briefly consider a less pleasant side of this matter.

In border regions strategic value is a necessary supplement to the highest requirements that any communications and transportation system might possess. That value can be measured, evaluated, and studied with a cold, technical eye and without any aggressive intent. In our day in America, such intent would not only be reprehensible but frankly ridiculous.

Let me, then, present the matter in unvarnished and matter-of-fact terms, my only rhetoric being of the sort that might be invoked to solve a problem in basic geometry.

Consider the general directions of the Purus, the Juruá and the Javari on the map and then those of the Madre de Dios and the Ucayali. The former group, in what we might term their uniform, equally spaced courses, deploy themselves like so many sectoring ditches; they subdivide the land. The last two are long, unifying ties; they encompass the land. Above its confluence with the Marañon, the Ucayali turns eight degrees to the south, then veers to the east as the Urubamba and, dividing into the Mishagua and the Serjali, almost anastomoses with the last of the westernmost sources of the Madre de Dios. That river, above the confluence of the Beni, which carries it on to the Madeira, breaks into an extensive network of curves that cut through seven degrees of longitude to the west; it then turns slightly to the north through the Manú thalweg and, dividing into the Caspajali and the Shauinto, almost meets the last western sources of the Ucayali. Between the two, a piece of ground a mere five miles wide: the Isthmus of Fitzcarrald. The two rivers thus encircle almost the entirety of Amazonia, an area of nearly 1,100,000 square kilometers, forming what, viewed this way, is the largest peninsula on earth.

That hydrographic picture is one of a huge pincers that encircle and grip a piece of continent in arms articulated at that isthmus.

It is a disposition that is highly unfavorable to the security and defense of our borders in that area.

Let me straightforwardly demonstrate the point.

Initially there seems to be the opposite illusion. If we hypothesize a conflict with the neighboring countries, we might at first glance place stock in the incomparable value of those three or four extensive roads. Entering by the Purus, by the Acre, by the Juruá, and even by the Javari, four expeditionary forces could be mobilized and could establish multiple other points quite distant from each other in a 700-kilometer swath of operations extending from the northeast to the southwest. Indeed, those watercourses recall the strategic routes of the Roman "consular ways." They bisect the border forcefully, in perpendicular.

That effect is, however, canceled out by the huge surround of the Madre de Dios-Ucayali combination.

A simple contrast of the geometrical positions is revealing.

In point of fact, the perpendicular deployment of our avenues of access, striking the border area head-on and cutting straight across it, contrasts with the parallel relationship between the border and the two enormous rivers that embrace it.

Hence this corollary: the necessarily distant end points that would be our objectives at the end of river navigation would represent for our adversaries mere points along their lines of operation. To guarantee ourselves a given number of positions we would need that same number of combat units and each would have to make that perpendicular journey. The adversaries, by contrast, with a few light, shallow-draft launches could defend all of our points of entrance at once.

In the case of fortunate outcome, victory on our part would have had to do with conquering on the field of combat. For them, it would be in delaying the outcome. Defeated at any of our isolated points without lateral connections with our other forces, we would have it as our only recourse to retreat, leaving that point of entry open to invasion. The opponent, if he is beaten at one point, can re-form in lightning remobilizations by moving back to the Pachitea by means of the Ucayali, or to the Inambari by means of the Madre de Dios.

These are undeniable conclusions. They are summarized by yet another, higher one that synthesizes them all. It is that, apart from the hypothesis of a daring offensive against the foreign country, the expeditionary forces on the Juruá, the Purus, and the Acre, once they arrive at their distant destinations, are condemned to immobility—put in reactive positions, unable to surveille the stretches of forest that separate them. By contrast, the Ucayali and the Madre de Dios, from Nauta to the Isthmus of Fitzcarrald and from there to the mouth of the Beni, are roads that offer no impediment to ongoing patrols and generalized control.

Such different resources are not even comparable. Those last two rivers, in their rapid linking of all the elements of resistance and in facilitating the most complex mobilizations, constitute an unmatched military roadway.

Now, a rail line from Cruzeiro do Sul to the Acre would counter that position of superiority.

Oriented, as it would be, as the cord of that enormous enveloping curve, it would possess some of its same features thus counterbalance its effect.

Demonstration is unnecessary. The geographical image is in and of itself sufficiently indicative.

Beyond this, what should be seen in that projected rail line is, above all else, a great international avenue of civilizing alliance and of peace.

Notes

1. For example, even Dr. H. Schnoor, a master who has constructed more than two thousand kilometers of rail line, in a recent discussion at the Engineering Club about the technical conditions of the Madeira-Mamoré, did

not hesitate to advise a 0.6-meter gauge; 10-kilogram rails, Decauville type; 20-ton locomotives, 5 percent grades, and 20-meter-radius curves.

These are his exact words: "In my judgment it will be necessary to move ahead laying the track, pushing on in whatever way possible, building wood bridges instead of the complete finished product, in order to then build the final version after the line is laid" (*Revista do Clube de Engenharia* 7, no. 11 [1905]).

2. This great avenue, at its greatest development, will have a surface of 726,000 meters by 40 meters, or 29,040,000 square meters. Allowing the high-end rate of 50 reis per square meter (twice the amount that Dr. Chrockatt de Sá budgeted for the Madeira-Marmoré), its opening would cost only 1,452,000,000 reis.

Glossary

arroba   Old measurement, equivalent to 14.7 kilograms.

bandeirante   A man who took part in a *bandeira* (flag) expedi-
                      tion during colonial times. *Bandeira* expeditions
                      originated in São Paulo and traveled west, north,
                      and south enslaving Indians and looking for pre-
                      cious minerals.

barracão   House where the owner of a rubber plantation
                      lived. It also served as a warehouse for the rubber
                      collected by the tappers and as a shop where the
                      rubber tappers were obliged to buy their everyday
                      goods.

caboclo   Indian–white mestizo.

casa do paricá   Among the Mura and the Mawé, the house where
                      the ritual of *paricá* was held. *Paricá* was a narcotic
                      substance derived from the fruit of the *paricá* tree.
                      The fruit was reduced to ashes by burning and then
                      inhaled in rituals held in a special house, hence *casa
                      do paricá.*

Castiloa	Short for the scientific name for *caucho*, *Castilloa ulei*.
cauchero	Collector of *caucho*.
caucho	Rubber collected from the *Castilloa ulei*. Collection involves felling the tree.
Cearense	From the state of Ceará in the Northeast of Brazil.
chicha	Alcoholic beverage made from fermented manioc, corn, or fruit.
cholo/a	Person of indigenous origin.
estancia	Farm or rural house.
firmes	Higher lands.
furo	Water path through vegetation that serves as a link between rivers.
Hevea	Short for the scientific name of the rubber tree *Hevea brasiliensis*.
igapó	Region of the Amazon that remains flooded during the dry season.
igarapé	A stream that originates in the forest and runs toward a river.
jagunço	A bandit or violent man from the *sertão*.
maloca	Native house.
mondongo	Low, swampy land covered with vegetation.
Paraibano	From the state of Paraíba in the Northeast of Brazil.

peón (Spanish)	Worker.
puesto cauchero (Spanish)	A center where *caucho* is stored and negotiated.
sacado	Lake that forms during the Amazon flooding season near the banks of big rivers.
salão (pl. *salões*)	Lowland that has become virtually impermeable to water.
seringa	Rubber from *Hevea brasiliensis*. It is collected from small cuts made in the bark of the tree, which is not felled.
seringueiro	Rubber tapper.
sernambi	Low-quality rubber that coagulates in the bowl before it is processed.
sertanejo/a	Person from the *sertão*.
sertão	Drought-ridden territory in the interior of the Brazilian Northeast.
tambo	Rustic house with thatched roof.
tejúpar	House made of palm leaves.
torrão (pl. *torrões*)	Clay lowland.
várzea	Flood plain.

Bibliography

Bosi, Alfredo. *História concisa da literatura brasileira*. São Paulo: Cultrix, 1970.

Carvajal, Fray Gaspar de. 1992. *Relación del nuevo descubrimiento del Rio Grande de las amazonas*. Quito: Comisión Nacional Permanente de Conmemoraciones Cívicas/Museo Antropológico del Banco Central de Guayaquil.

Cunha, Euclides da. *Obra completa*, Vol. 1. Rio: Aguilar, 1966.

———. *Um paraíso perdido: Reunião dos ensaios amazônicos*. Edited by Hildon Rocha. Rio: Vozes, 1976.

———. *Rebellion in the Backlands [Os Sertões]*. Translated by Samuel Putnam. Chicago: University of Chicago Press, 1944.

Freyre, Gilberto. "Euclides da Cunha. Revelador da realidade brasileira." In Euclides da Cunha, *Obra completa*, 1:17–31. Rio: Aguilar, 1966.

Hardman, Francisco Foot. "A vingança da Hiléia: Os sertões amazônicos de Euclides." *Revista Tempo Brasileiro* 144 (2001): 29–61. Special number: *Repensando o Brasil com Euclides da Cunha*.

Lauria, Márcio José. "Judas-Ahsverus." In *Enciclopédia de estudos Euclidianos*. Vol. 1. Jundiaí: Jundiá, 1982.

Lima, Luiz Costa. "Os Sertões: Ciência ou literatura?" *Revista Tempo Brasileiro* 144 (2001). Special number: *Repensando o Brasil com Euclides da Cunha*.

———. *Terra Incógnita: a construção de os sertões*. Rio: Civilização Brasileira, 1997.

Magalhães, José Vieira Couto de. *O Selvagem*. Rio: Magalhães, 1913.

Rodrigues, João Barbosa. *Poranduba amazonense ou kochyma uara porandub: 1872–1887*. Rio: Leuzinger, 1890.

Rosaldo, Renato. *Culture and Truth. The Remaking of Social Analysis.* Boston: Beacon, 1993.

Stokes, Charles. "The Acre Revolutions, 1899–1903: A Study in Brazilian Expansionism." Ph.D. diss., Tulane University, 1974.

Stradelli, Ermanno. *La leggenda dell'jurupary e outras lendas amazónicas.* Caderno 4. São Paulo: Instituto Cultural Italo-Brasileiro, 1964.

Tocantins, Leandro. *Euclides da Cunha e o paraíso perdido.* Rio: Civilização Brasileira, 1978.

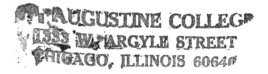